The True Gold Standard

Selected publications by
Lewis E. Lehrman and sponsored by
The Lehrman Institute

The Atlantic Alliance and Its Critics
by Robert Tucker et al

Balance of Power or Hegemony: The Interwar Monetary System
edited by Benjamin M. Rowland

China: American Financial Colony or Mercantilist Predator
by Lewis E. Lehrman

The Dollar Problem and Its Solution
by Lewis E. Lehrman

Gold in a Global Multi-Asset Portfolio
by Lewis E. Lehrman

Lincoln at Peoria: The Turning Point
by Lewis E. Lehrman

Monetary Policy, the Federal Reserve, and Gold
by Lewis E. Lehrman

Money and the Coming World Order
by Charles Kindleberger, Lewis E. Lehrman, et al

Oeuvres Complètes de Jacques Rueff
edited by Emil-Marie Claasen and Georges Lane

*Protectionism, Inflation, or Monetary Reform: The Case for Fixed
Exchange Rates and a Modernized Gold Standard*
by Lewis E. Lehrman

The Purposes of American Power: An Essay on National Security
by Robert Tucker

*U.S.-Japanese Economic Relations:
Cooperation, Competition, and Confrontation*
by Diane Tasca

For more information about the author, Lewis E. Lehrman,

or the work of The Lehrman Institute,

please visit **www.LehrmanInstitute.org.**

To keep abreast of the latest on *The True Gold Standard*,

please visit **www.TheGoldStandardNow.org** where additional

information, breaking news, and research on monetary policy,

economics, and the gold standard may be found.

Front Cover: The eagle on the cover rests watchfully from its parapet on the façade of the Federal Reserve Building in Washington. Pursuant to Article I, Section 8 of the Constitution, Congress passed the Coinage Act of 1792. Many of the Founders and the signers of the Constitution participated. The Coinage Act defined the dollar as a weight unit of gold and silver, establishing thereby the *gold eagle* as a ten dollar gold coin for circulation among the people.

Symbolically, the granite eagle on the façade of the Fed has been given its gold patina by the editors of this book.

The True Gold Standard

A Monetary Reform Plan
without Official Reserve Currencies

How We Get from Here to There

Lewis E. Lehrman
August 15, 2011

ISBN-10: 0-9840178-0-1
ISBN-13: 978-0-9840178-0-5

Published by The Lehrman Institute
www.LehrmanInstitute.org

Printed in the United States

First Edition, Second Printing

For my children and my children's children.

For every American whose freedom, prosperity, and security depend on a stable dollar.

Let them inherit a stable monetary standard worthy of a free people.

"If the gold standard could be reintroduced..., we all believe that the reform would promote trade and production like nothing else, but also stimulate international credit and transfers of capital to the places where they are most useful. One of the greatest elements of uncertainty would be suppressed."

— John Maynard Keynes
Commercial Manchester Guardian
Reconstruction Supplement
April 20, 1922

Contents

Illustrations

Summary of the Monetary Reform Plan

America and the world need a twenty-first century international gold standard. America should lead by unilateral resumption of the gold monetary standard. Unilateral resumption means that the United States dollar will be defined in federal statute as a certain weight unit of gold. The Treasury, the Federal Reserve System, and the banking system will be responsible for maintaining the gold value of the United States dollar.

All financial claims on banks and government agencies, chartered or supervised under federal law, that are payable in dollars shall be redeemable in gold at the statutory rate without restriction—demand deposits (e.g. checking accounts) to be redeemed upon demand but other dollar claims at maturity. Americans will be free to use gold and authorized, mint-issued, gold coins as money without restriction or the threat of taxation. The Treasury and authorized private mints will provide for the minting of legal tender gold coins, to be used as money, without restriction or taxation. The Board of Governors of the Federal

Reserve or any successor institution serving in a similar capacity, and all banks chartered or supervised by the United States government, or any one of its agencies, will be obliged by law to sustain the statutory dollar-gold parity and to redeem Federal Reserve notes and bank demand deposits for gold on demand.

To facilitate termination of the dollar-based reserve currency system, American authorities will invite interested nations to a conference to establish a modernized international gold standard. By international gold standard it is meant that only gold—not dollars, nor any other currency, nor so-called Special Drawing Rights (SDR)—would be the means by which nations settle their residual balance-of-payments deficits.

Lewis E. Lehrman
August 15, 2011

Introduction

The outline of this Monetary Reform Plan was developed in the 1970s, discussed extensively with President Reagan in 1983, and spelled out in books, essays, and op-ed pieces for several decades. Today, I submit this urgent proposal to my fellow Americans and our friends abroad because the historical evidence of the early twentieth century compels me to believe that contemporary international monetary disorder, national currency wars, and inflationary impoverishment of working people the world over has again led to violent social disorder, revolutionary civil strife, and vicious deflationary consequences. Natural resource rivalry, competitive currency depreciations, mercantilism, and war clouds have appeared together from time immemorial.

In previous centuries, world financial disintegration has often preceded civil wars, national wars of revenge, indeed catastrophic global war in certain cases. American national security risks are *now* high and rising. Therefore, *now* is the time to restore monetary order, to end inflation, and to restore a stable dollar and stable exchange rates—in order to create global incentives for peaceful, equitable, growing world trade—and with these incentives recreate worldwide rising standards of living.

The True Gold Standard responds to a constant question: how precisely does the United States once again establish a stable dollar worth its weight in gold? How do the United States, and other countries, get from *here* to *there*? These questions have been raised and debated at crucial junctures over the last century— after the creation of the Federal Reserve System in 1913, followed by the catastrophe of World War I; after Franklin Roosevelt in 1933 nationalized all gold holdings; after August 15, 1971, when President Nixon severed the last weak link between the dollar and gold; and, most recently, after the Great Recession of 2007-09 marked by the open-ended subsidies by the Federal Reserve System and the Treasury to the privileged and cartelized world banking system.

Over the last century, the value of the dollar has declined dramatically, as evidenced in Figure 1.

After almost a century of manipulated paper- and credit-based currencies, how do nations, which need the benefits of free trade in order to prosper, terminate the anarchy of volatile,

Figure 1. Decline in the Dollar's Value, 1910-2011

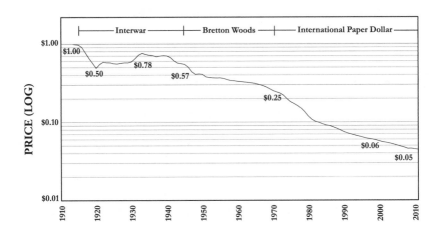

Sources and Notes: The price of one ounce of gold in March 1910 was $20 and, on August 15, 2011, on the date of publication of this book, the price was $1,740. Different monetary regimes are identified, as follows: the international gold standard from 1879-1914; the gold-exchange standard or interwar monetary standard from 1914-1944; the Bretton Woods system from 1944-1971; and, the international paper dollar standard from 1971 through the present day. (See also Appendix III.)

depreciating, floating exchange rates? *Free trade without stable exchange rates is a fantasy.*

Since the inauguration of Bretton Woods in 1944, so-called free trade has been maintained and subsidized by the especially open market and overvalued reserve currency dollar of the United States. Because of pegged exchange rates to the dollar under

Bretton Woods, overvaluation of the dollar was an ineluctable result of the excess demand for the sole reserve currency—the dollar. Most developing countries and other developed countries understood the perversity of the dollar's reserve currency role. Some of them have protected their markets with undervalued currencies, quotas, and regulations—China most egregiously in recent years. But in the post-World War II Bretton Woods monetary system, United States sponsorship of free trade made the wide open market of American industry an easy target for mercantilists worldwide to mobilize undervalued currencies to build growing export machines without giving commensurate reciprocity to the United States—the General Agreement on Tariffs and Trade (GATT) and World Trade Organization (WTO) notwithstanding.

In a word, since World War II, free trade has often been at the expense of United States businesses, manufacturing, and labor.

How, therefore, may America now lead other nations toward an equitable and renewed world trading system based on a new monetary order, stable exchange rates, and reciprocal free trade inuring to the mutual benefit of all? How do the same nations stage the resumption of a true gold standard, without the escalating debt and leverage of official reserve currencies?

How do American authorities and free market participants use market-oriented techniques to establish the optimum gold value of the dollar and stable exchange rates, such that the durability of the gold standard and the stability of the general price level is assured over the long run? What are some desirable reforms of the central and commercial banking system—to be induced by market and government adaptations to the termination of the paper dollar's role as an official reserve currency? What collateral banking reforms might be necessary to limit the excesses of the present, government-subsidized, fractional-reserve banking system such that prudent banking, under strict fiduciary rules, would reinforce, not destabilize, the long-term durability of a stable gold dollar?

The True Gold Standard endeavors to answer these questions.

American leadership is hard work. American leadership on monetary reform will be hard work. We should have no illusions about the degree of difficulty posed by the necessity of comprehensive reform. Neither did the Founders in the revolutionary crisis, nor General Washington at the birth of the Republic, nor General Eisenhower contemplating D-Day, nor Prime Minister Churchill at the Battle of Britain. We Americans have been here before. We can do this work and win.

America must now take one of two divergent roads. *First,* America may persist on the road of soft indulgence afforded by the unstable dollar's official reserve currency role—the enabler of ever-rising budget and balance-of-payments deficits, therefore of immense American foreign debt. (See Figures 2 and 3.) Though the centrality of the world dollar standard may gradually decline, it may still continue for another generation because of the unique amplitude and liquidity of the dollarized financial markets, repositories for vast sums not easily stored elsewhere as official national reserves. Therefore, the "exorbitant privilege" of the dollar's role as the world's primary reserve currency may enable American authorities, policy makers, and academic economists to persist in rationalizing the misleading mask of this reserve currency privilege as a boon, instead of a deadly economic malignancy leading ultimately to national insolvency.

Or, *second,* American leaders may acknowledge the dollar's

world reserve currency role as an insupportable burden, instead of a privilege. It is a burden because decades of supplying dollar reserves to the world in the form of dollar debt has caused an exponentially rising burden of United States foreign and domestic debt. This process enables America to finance rising American budget and balance-of-payments deficits without institutional limits. These monetized deficits of the reserve currency country entail arbitrage mechanisms which cause inflation followed by deflation both at home and abroad.

If American leaders continue to choose *option one*—rising debt and deficits financed by the dollar's reserve currency role— the reserve currency fantasy may carry on for several more decades before its complete collapse. Historians have analyzed the very same pattern of gradual reserve currency decline of the British imperial pound as it persisted after World War II—lingering as it did on life support for three more decades, then collapsing, finally making clear to the world the general collapse of British power (Barnett 1986).

If American leaders choose *option two*, they will reject the siren song of the reserve currency's "exorbitant privilege." They will acknowledge the insupportable burden of the dollar's official reserve currency role. They will plan now for the termination and wind up of the dollar's reserve currency role, restore dollar convertibility to gold, define by statute the dollar as a certain weight unit of gold, and propose gold as the sole international reserve currency, thereafter settling all residual balance-of-payments deficits in gold alone.

This book, *The True Gold Standard, A Monetary Reform Plan without Official Reserve Currencies*, focuses primarily on option two—*How We Get from Here to There*.

For America to choose *option one* is not unlike an intelligent, insouciant dare-devil, Icarus, who—well-suited for the leap—takes off from the fiftieth floor of his skyscraper, secure in the knowledge that he is feeling fine ten floors down, the street level still forty floors far below.

To choose *option two* is to choose the American Constitutional roadmap to monetary reconstruction on the bedrock of a stable dollar, shorn of the crushing weight of trade disadvantages and the accumulating dollar debt intensified by the reserve currency system.

American monetary and economic reconstruction on this historic basis will lead to a resurgence of rapid economic growth empowered by a sound and stable dollar and the renewed confidence and certainty born of market expectations of a stable long-term price level. These fundamental incentives will engender a vast increase of true savings available for long-term investment from current income—investable savings—and much more from dishoarding. The outpouring of savings will be redeployed by entrepreneurs in new and innovative plants, technology, and equipment, minimizing unemployment as skilled and unskilled workers are hired to manage the new facilities. The United States export production machine will be reoriented to the world market under free and fair trading conditions.

This is the true road of American monetary and economic reconstruction.

I offer this Monetary Reform Plan to assist in such an historic American renaissance, hoping that the Plan itself will be perfected by colleagues, critics, and far-seeing American leaders.

* * * * * * * * *

Although for this policy piece I have excluded footnotes, almost every issue considered here—both in the affirmative and on the negative—is thoroughly debated in the several monographs and articles listed in the selected bibliography. This plan is an extended essay, not an econometric exercise. Limited by space, the tables and graphs are few in number, believing those chosen to illuminate the subject considered. The arguments and proposals for each subject considered are confined to separate sections—sometimes short. I attempt to make each section stand alone so it does not depend for its coherence on a reading of the entire manuscript. There is, as a result, inevitable repetition.

The Purpose of *The True Gold Standard*

This Monetary Reform Plan proposes to establish the framework for an enduring, stable value for the United States dollar; that is, to define the dollar by statute as a certain weight unit of gold to be coined into lawful money.

Long associated with free market prices, mobile factors of production, and free people, a "dollar convertible to gold"* is warranted by the United States Constitution in Article I, Sections 8 and 10. (See Appendix I.) A monetary standard of precious metal (gold and silver) was the institutional monetary foundation, the gyroscope of the great Industrial Revolution of the western world, giving rise at the birth of the American Republic to a reasonably stable American currency. Wars did interrupt stability and growth. But over the long run, economic productivity and population expansion led to unprecedented prosperity. They were hallmarks of the United States from the Coinage Act of

---

* The term "convertibility" is a conventional but misleading usage handed down from time immemorial. I use the term reluctantly. The historic dollar of the American Constitution should be understood as a certain weight unit of precious metal. Paper and credit monies should be no more than rights to redemption in gold dollars at the statutory parity.

1792 (see Appendix II) until 1971 when the last vestige of dollar linkage to gold was suspended. Floating paper money exchange rates, mixed with pegged and manipulated exchange rates, have persisted during peace and war to this very day. (Since 1971 average hourly real wages have hardly improved.)

A floating, or pegged, paper and credit currency has proven itself throughout history an unreliable, depreciating store of value. Unlike the paper dollar, a dollar defined in law as a weight unit of gold is the monetary standard which simultaneously provides all the primary functions of true standard money: (1) a stable store of value; (2) a stable measure and unit-of-account; and, (3) a universally accepted means of payment. A gold monetary standard combines, in one monetary article of wealth, the three primary functions of money. Moreover, the true gold standard of history provides the global networking effects of universally acceptable, equitable, ubiquitous, standard money. Through long historical evolution gold became free trade money.

Throughout ancient and modern history it was *the unique properties of the gold monetary standard* which made it universally acceptable to trading peoples in the market. The test of what will endure as honest money can only be studied in the empirical laboratory of human history; mathematical abstractions, drawn from the blackboards of academic economists, will not do. Because trust and universal acceptability are the trademarks of honest money—these virtues must be affirmed, in the long run, by the tests of the open market, and then reinforced by wise, limited, and prudent governments which understand and embrace the inductive, tested verdict of the market.

No perfect monetary system can be fashioned in this imperfect world, peopled by imperfect human beings. But the natural monetary properties of the true gold standard—developed by supple and subtle institutional mechanisms through centuries of observation and experience—provide the world trading system with the least imperfect domestic and international monetary system. Such a system best enables that fragile reed known as civilization to endure.

The Properties of Gold

Gold is a fundamental, metallic element of the earth's chemical constitution. Gold exhibits unique properties which have enabled it, through two millennia of testing, to emerge as universally accepted money. In the Periodic Table of Elements, *gold is one of a class of substances that consists solely of atoms of the same atomic number. Its essential composition reveals perfect integrity, homogeneity, and fungibility.* Rarely considered in monetary debates, these natural properties of gold enabled it to prevail over the long run in the market as universally acceptable money by means of which to make exchanges for all other articles of wealth. Thus, the preference of ancient and modern civilizations to use gold as money was no mere accident of history. Nor has this natural preference for gold been easily purged by government fiat.

Consider the natural properties of gold. Gold is durable, homogenous, and fungible. Indeed, by its intrinsic nature, gold is imperishable, indestructible, and malleable. Gold is portable and can be readily transported from place to place in exchange for other articles of wealth. Large and small quantities of gold can be safely stored in exchange for redeemable certificates and notes. Like paper, gold is almost infinitely divisible into smaller denominations. But, unlike the zero marginal cost of producing paper money, gold—like other articles of wealth in the market—requires real labor and capital to be produced. Paper money of zero marginal cost is, therefore, overproduced—tending rapidly or gradually toward worthlessness whereas gold sustains stable purchasing power over the centuries (Jastram 1977).

Because of its imperishability, gold can be held or stored permanently. Gold survived centuries of monetary experiments with perishable alternatives such as grains, cattle, tobacco, and many other monetary tokens which are neither long lasting, nor storable for long periods, nor portable over long distances to exchange for other goods and to settle debts. A single ounce of gold is a densely packed elemental value drawn from the earth's crust, its relative scarcity and desirability sustained not least because of the cost of real factors of production required to produce it. Because of these natural properties gold was, and remains, universally acceptable in the market as a reliable store of value over the long run.

Merchants, bankers, farmers, laborers and traders may not have self-consciously considered these facts, but they behaved as if they did. People freely accepted gold, from generation to generation, in exchange for other goods because gold money could be held as a store of stable future purchasing power. That is, the gold monetary standard was a stable proxy for a basket of goods and services to be purchased later, perhaps much later—a methodological precursor, drawn from nature, of the Consumer Price Index (CPI). Historical data confirm that gold money preserves its purchasing power over the long run—as inconvertible paper and credit money do not.

The global monetary stock of above-ground gold today approximates five- to six-billion ounces—approximately one ounce per capita, similar to the proportion of past centuries. Because of gold's preeminent lasting value from time immemorial, and the incentive to conserve it, these five- to six-billion ounces of above ground gold represent almost all of the gold ever produced. They are, *en masse*, easily stored as reserves for safekeeping by individuals, banks, and governments. So densely packed is the value of gold that today the above ground gold stock may be enclosed in a cube of approximately seventy (70) feet on each side.

The empirical data of monetary history also demonstrate that the stock of above ground gold has grown for centuries in direct proportion to the growth of population and output per capita. As with all desired goods and services in the market, discovery, intelligence, and work lead over the long run to the production of sufficient growth of the desired gold stock by which to accommodate economic growth and a stable long-term price level. The stable long-run growth of the gold stock was a fundamental reason why the true gold standard was the stable institutional monetary foundation associated with the extraordinary economic and population growth of the vast Industrial Revolution of the nineteenth century.

Over the long run, the quantity of gold in circulation tends to grow directly in proportion to population growth and growth of output per capita. This ineluctable fact underlies nature's hidden equation which caused the market freely to select gold as the least imperfect monetary standard for market exchange, stable long-run growth, and a stable price level. As the technology of the payments mechanism evolved—bringing bank notes, checks, and the use of wires (among other credit and monetary transfer mechanisms) into monetary circulation—these substitute monetary tokens derived their value and utility because, at the time of their origin and subsequently, they were rights or claims to a stable, defined weight unit of precious metal—primarily gold during and after the nineteenth century Industrial Revolution. Despite the legal tender disabilities presently imposed by the political authorities, gold retains today the same inherent properties which make it the optimal, stable money of the market over the long run. *What remains to be done is to define the dollar again as a certain weight unit of gold.*

In a word, gold is natural money—not least because it combines in a single indestructible substance the three primary functions of money enumerated above. Thus did gold become the uniform monetary weight and measure in the market. By combining the three essential functions of money into one stable and imperishable monetary token, the market and then the authorities bestowed on gold the status of an official monetary standard endowed with the profound national and international networking benefits of economies of scale—essential characteristics of a world standard.

Academic economists, policy makers, and intellectual elites are indifferent to the fact that gold is universally desired by men and women for its beauty. Throughout history, gold has been freely desired in the market not only as money but also for adornment (a form of durable saving); and, for special industrial uses because of its unique chemical properties. That gold is desired and beheld by all as beautiful constitutes a monetary virtue, an aesthetic judgment acknowledged freely in almost all civilizations and cultures.

Restoration of the Gold Dollar

I. Aims and Effects

Restoration of the gold dollar aims at long-term goals: increased saving and investment in productive facilities, rising employment and real wages joined to a stable price level—reinforced by stable exchange rates, and a stable, unsubsidized banking system. To these ends, the gold value of the dollar would be established by law at a level such that the level of average wages do not fall, ruling out deflationary effects—for example, the failed British restoration of convertibility in 1925 after World War I. The more successful French restorations of 1926 and 1959 are useful examples (Rueff 1964). *In today's context the methodology for market discovery and establishment of the optimum gold value of the dollar is explained on pages 51-86.*

The permanent value of the gold dollar is intended to underwrite, among other things, just and lasting compensation for workers, savers, and investors; to prevent distortions in relative prices by manipulated paper currencies and floating exchange rates which unjustly and unwisely misallocate scarce resources;

and, to promote long-term savings and rising real wages paid in dollars convertible to gold. A gold dollar restrains political and banking authorities such that they cannot lawfully depreciate the present value or the long-term purchasing power of dollar wages, savings, and fixed incomes through government-caused inflation—nor capriciously cause major inflations or paper money debt deflations.

A stable dollar leads to increased saving both from income and dishoarding—releasing a vast reservoir of savings hoarded in commodities, art, and other vehicles purchased to protect against the threat of inflation. The release of these savings, imprisoned by fear and inflation, are mobilized by entrepreneurs and managers into new income-generating investment and productive facilities leading to increased employment needed to sustain them. Thus does growth through consistent and increasing long-term capital investment per capita, based on a stable monetary standard, sustain prosperity, rising real wages, long-term employment and consumption. On the other hand, consumption through increasing government debt finance, transfer payments, and paper money fiscal stimulation suppresses investment, erodes entrepreneurial confidence, engenders both credit inflation and credit deflation, ultimately ending in tears.

With the long-term stability of the gold dollar established, a major economic mutation evolves. Two generations of worldwide hoarding for safety from paper money inflation and deflation gradually comes to an end. Hoarding in the form of gold, antiques, art, commodities, diamonds, jewelry, and innumerable other vehicles—in order to escape depreciating currencies—will give way to the new reality of a stable gold dollar—the authentic monetary store of value. People worldwide will have regained the confidence to exchange non-income and income-producing inflation hedges for convertible currencies with which to invest for the long-term in superior income-producing facilities—also thereby in working capital commitments for new employment.

Confidence in the long-term stable purchasing power of a gold dollar will lead to more public investment in new infrastructure and more entrepreneurial production of new products and services. Demand for skilled and unskilled labor to implement more labor-intensive, long-term, public infrastructure and private manufacturing will be intensified, mobilized in the wake of the vast new increase of savings from income and dishoarding. Reckless credit and debt inflation is replaced by real savings.

The road to full employment will have been reconstructed.

A crucial element of this Monetary Reform Plan is designed to bring about, by market mechanisms, a wide circulation of gold coins as legal tender so that the sovereign people, not elite bankers and unaccountable political authorities, control the quantity of money in circulation. *Because market participants are at liberty to redeem bank demand deposits and paper currency for gold at the legally established parity, central bank issue of new money and credit to finance government budget deficits and insolvent banks is strictly limited. Banks unable, according to law, to redeem demand deposits in gold at the statutory parity would become insolvent or be merged with prudent competitors.*

Another primary aim of this Plan is to limit inflation and deflation by appropriate institutional reforms of the monetary and banking system. Ultimately, inflation is caused by: (1) direct and indirect Federal Reserve financing and refinancing of escalating government spending and the budget deficit; and, (2) the perverse workings of official reserve currency systems which enable and sustain the permanent balance-of-payments deficits of the reserve currency countries—primarily the United States since World War II. (For an illustration of the ever-growing national budget and balance-of-payments deficits, see Figures 2 and 3.)

The United States balance-of-payments deficits have been financed since the end of World War II by foreign central bank purchases of the flood of excess dollars going abroad. Today this process has been intensified by quantitative easing, a euphemism for central bank money printing or credit creation. Once abroad, these excess dollars are monetized by foreign monetary authorities as official foreign exchange reserves. But the foreign dollar reserves are then reinvested in the United States dollar market, substantially in United States government securities sold to finance the federal budget deficit. In effect, the United States receives back the money it appeared to give up to make payments abroad. Thus, the world dollar standard enables America to buy without paying. This perverse mechanism, whereby the reserve currency country issues its own money to finance and refinance its deficits and debts increases potential global purchasing power,

Figure 2. Budget Deficits

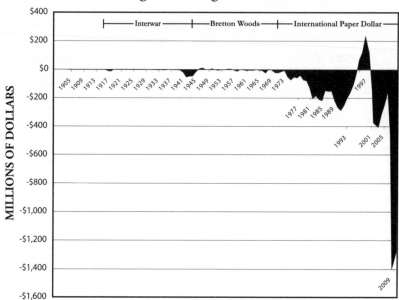

Sources and Notes: Data drawn from the Office of Management and Budget, United States White House, accessed on February 20, 2011.

creating a demand for goods and assets without producing an increased supply of them—leading, of course, to inflation at home and abroad.

This Monetary Reform Plan proposes to rule out the use of official reserve currencies to settle balance-of-payments deficits. The Plan proposes to substitute gold as the international settlements currency, effectively eliminating a root cause of global inflation because deficits must then be promptly settled—not in

Figure 3. Balance-of-Payments Deficits

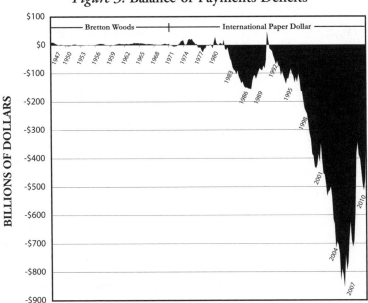

Sources and Notes: Data drawn from the Bureau of Economic Analysis, United States Department of Commerce, accessed on May 26, 2011.

newly issued national paper and credit monies, but in gold. The Plan forestalls, by law and by associated agreements, the financing of the United States government budget deficit and United States balance-of-payments deficit through new credit and money issued by the Federal Reserve, commercial banks, or by foreign central banks. By means of statutory convertibility, the Plan disciplines and limits the contemporary, unrestrained, credit-creating banking system, thus limiting the increase of government spending. Furthermore, by means of prompt settlement in gold of balance-of-payments deficits, equilibrium among trading partners is sustained and debt leverage diminished.

Terminating the reserve currency role of the dollar ends the insupportable burden borne by the United States. The United States no longer must go even further into debt in order to supply the world with necessary and desired reserves. (See Figure 2.) Moreover, terminating the "exorbitant privilege" of the world paper dollar standard brings to an end this essential cause of inflation and depreciation; and also ends these same risks to the reserves of foreign monetary authorities.

Institutional agreements to end the official reserve currency role of the dollar, and to limit discretionary Federal Reserve and banking system money issuance, effectively reinforce unrestricted convertibility of the currency. In general, unstable mutations in the true gold standard—including the "gold-exchange standard" of the 1920s and 1930s, the liquidation of which served as a primary cause of financial collapse and the intensification of the Great Depression—are ruled out. So, too, are pure, paper- and credit-based reserve currency systems.

In particular, this Monetary Reform Plan remedies the defects of the dollar-based, post-Second World War, official reserve currency system—an unsustainable system of currencies loosely pegged to the dollar and ineffectively linked to gold. The dollar-leveraged Bretton Woods pegged exchange rate system collapsed in 1971. The collapse ushered in the worst American economic decade since the 1930s, leading to an unemployment rate in 1982 higher even than the unemployment occasioned by the financial panic, deflation, and collapse of 2007-09.

Since 1971, the world dollar standard has been an even more perverse and crisis prone system than that of the Bretton Woods era (1944-71). During the past forty years, the privilege and the burden of the dollar's dominant and overvalued role as the world's official reserve currency has been a cause not only of inflation, but also of deindustrialization in the United States.

The perennial United States balance-of-payments deficit floods foreign financial systems and central banks with undesired dollars. They are typically purchased by these central banks against the issue of new domestic money, tending to cause inflation *there*. So-called sterilization techniques are not fully effective. The excess dollars purchased by foreign central banks are then reinvested in, among other dollar claims, United States government securities, thereby financing rising government spending and budget deficits, tending to cause inflation *here*.

Thus, the reserve currency system leads to a rapid increase in global purchasing power without a commensurate increase in the supply of goods and services. The systemic tendency of the reserve currency system is inflation—either in the prices of goods and services or in the prices of investment assets caused by hedging against Federal Reserve monetary policy and inflation. Yet the process can dangerously work in reverse to cause deflation, especially when the Fed tightens and global illiquidity causes foreign official dollar reserves to be resold or liquidated in very large quantities—as occurred in 1929-33 and recently in 2007-09. Figure 4 considers Parkinson's debt corollary, demonstrating the increased purchasing power generated by the reserve currency system—unassociated with a commensurate increase in the supply of goods and services.

Under this Plan, gold alone would replace the dollar as the world's official reserve currency. History shows that—in the

Figure 4. Parkinson's Debt Corollary

United States public debt expands to absorb all means of finance

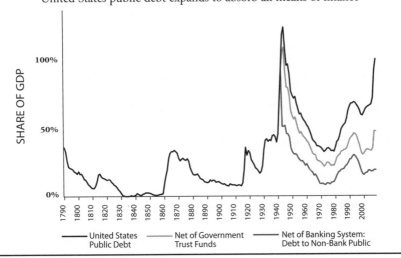

SHARE OF GDP

100%

50%

0%

1790 1800 1810 1820 1830 1840 1850 1860 1870 1880 1890 1900 1910 1920 1930 1940 1950 1960 1970 1980 1990 2000

——— United States   ——— Net of Government   ——— Net of Banking System:
Public Debt   Trust Funds   Debt to Non-Bank Public

Sources and Notes: Consider the striking evidence for Parkinson's debt corollary depicted above. At the end of fiscal year 2009, direct United States Treasury debt stood at some $11.9 trillion*, equal to about ninety percent (90%) of GDP. Of this amount, only about $2.2 trillion, or nineteen percent (19%), was held by the nonbank public, including foreigners. Some $5.3 trillion was held by federal, state, and local governments—mostly government pension funds like Social Security. The remainder, about $4.1 trillion, was held by the banking system. Of this amount, about $769 billion was held by the Federal Reserve and $122 billion by United States commercial banks and other depository institutions, while foreign monetary authorities held $3.6 trillion. Of this amount, $2.085 trillion was lent directly to the Treasury, $763 billion to government-sponsored agencies, and $709 billion indirectly through other official monetary liabilities. This latter expansion of means of financing United States public debt has driven the expansion of high-powered money; and since the Civil War, almost all of this credit has been extended to the Treasury.

All this demand for nonmonetary wealth without a matching supply necessarily pushes up the prices of securities or commodities—usually both in succession. Prices of stocks, bonds, and real estate are bid up immediately, and the real economy receives a temporary boost about a year later. If the process stopped there, the only permanent effect would be a rise in commodity prices, which typically (since the 1930s) takes about two and a half years.

The graph, sources, and notes were originally published by John D. Mueller in *Redeeming Economics* (2010).

* Today, total Federal direct debt including federal agency debt is $22 trillion.

absence of government prohibitions and restrictions in favor of inconvertible paper and credit money—gold, or paper and credit money convertible to gold, was preferred and accepted in trade and exchange from time immemorial. The gold standard underwrites the equilibrium mechanisms of the global economy which the world dollar standard has corrupted with increasing dollar debt and leverage at home and abroad. Under the world dollar standard, other nations gain desired reserves only as the United States becomes an increasingly leveraged debtor through balance-of-payments deficits; whereas under the gold standard, the global economy may attain balance-of-payments surplus as a whole vis-a-vis worldwide gold producers.

The Announcement of a proposed Monetary Reform Plan by the United States would be accompanied by invitations to an International Monetary Conference. Its overriding purpose would be to establish a new international monetary system—based on multilateral currency convertibility to gold—grounded in Treaty and national legislation. *Such a conference would not restrict America's freedom of action to proceed alone, if necessary, to gold convertibility of the dollar.* A stable dollar and stable currency exchange rates, all based on unrestricted currency convertibility to gold, would replace the financial disorder and mercantilism engendered by volatile floating exchange rates and the malignancy of pegged, undervalued currencies.

The Monetary Reform Plan suggests adaptations that free financial markets would tend spontaneously to induce over time as they adjusted to dollar convertibility to gold. Moreover, the Plan puts forward suggestions by which political and financial authorities might, over time, be guided to bring about desirable, market-oriented adjustments in the banking system by means of statutory and regulatory reform. Such rules would be intended to sustain the economic and social benefits of convertibility, reinforcing an enduring regime of stable money and stable exchange rates upon which to rebuild the trust and confidence necessary to facilitate the sustained economic growth engendered by an honest monetary standard. (See testimony of Lewis E. Lehrman before the United States Congress, House Committee on Financial Services, 2011.)

II. Means and Ends

A monetary regime based on the true gold standard is substantially self-regulating, creating a just, stable, integrated, and growing international trading and monetary system based on stable exchange rates and on a tested, impartial, non-national, common currency—*namely gold*. By empirical tests, *the true gold standard is the least imperfect monetary system by which to establish, over the long run, a stable dollar.* (See Appendix III.)

The United States Constitution warrants the restoration of the classical gold standard—that is to say, the true gold standard. (See Appendix I.) Empirical measures drawn from history— such as long-run stability of the general price level and average annual inflation rates over time combined with economic and employment growth—document the true (or classical) gold standard's success. No one should confuse the manipulated and deeply flawed, interwar gold-exchange standard (1922-44) or the equally flawed and unstable dollar-based Bretton Woods official reserve currency system (1944-71) with the true gold standard. Both arrangements followed the catastrophes of two world wars, taking the form of unstable official reserve currency systems. (See the *Age of Inflation* and the *Balance of Payments* by Jacques Rueff.)

Moreover, it is too often overlooked that before World War I the gold standard was the institutional monetary basis of the unique and remarkable economic growth of America and the western world during the Industrial Revolution. This commercial revolution raised much of early mankind from 50,000 years of Malthusian subsistence to the prosperity of sustained economic growth which got under way in the late eighteenth and nineteenth centuries—an economic revolution emulated over the past century by most developing nations of the world.

During the past two centuries, the secular growth of population, international trade, the spread of invention, and the rise of a prosperous, international middle class cannot be dissociated from its origins in an international economy characterized by stable exchange rates underwritten by the true gold standard. In this seminal period of human history, characterized by secular economic growth and sustained rising standards of living, currency convertibility to gold was an indispensable gyroscope of rapidly growing international trade (Clark 2008).

During this period, gold-based currencies were the

trustworthy monetary vehicles which grounded stable exchange rates, long-run economic confidence, increased savings and investment, and secured future growth of the domestic and international economy which sustained the Industrial Revolution. It must be emphasized that United States growth required global growth. But over the long run, global growth requires stable exchange rates, not currency wars born of floating and undervalued currencies. Global growth can for a generation or two be subsidized—by a singularly rich, hegemonic power like the British Empire or the United States by means of an overvalued currency and a wide open market for goods from other mercantilist countries; but eventually instability, decline, and the rise of protected competitors overtake the reserve currency regime.

In the long run, free trade without stable exchange rates is a fantasy.

Thus, the European and North American Agricultural and Industrial Revolutions cannot be dissociated from their trustworthy monetary basis—the true gold standard era. The Industrial Revolution was a breakaway era from all earlier periods of human economic activity during which human population, prosperity, and economic growth experienced Malthusian cycles of rise, decline, and fall—generally enforced by scarcity of food and fuel which did not grow sufficiently to feed and support secular growth in the population (Clark 2008).

During the Industrial Revolution, mutually gold convertible national paper- and credit-based currencies were the guide posts of early modern trading nations which thereby balanced their trade and payments as they grew out of subsistence.

A. Monetary Reform and the General Price Level

A gold-based currency stabilizes the long-term price level (Jastram 1977). It restores the necessary confidence for long-term private and public savings and increasing investment per capita— indispensable for increasing real wages, growing prosperity, and the tendency to full employment. As the savings rate and investment per capita increase, productivity and real wages are thereby increased—and sustained without inflation. Moreover, the dissipation of inflation hedges (dishoarding) releases immense liquid savings for capital investment, replacing excessive credit and debt leverage.

Adoption of the true gold standard is necessary to reform the flawed financial institutions which gave rise in the past century (1914-2011) to perennial international payments imbalances and to destabilizing budget deficits in national public finances. These disorders have also included: an exponential increase in government spending, engendered by central bank financing of government budget deficits; and flawed gold-exchange standards and official reserve currencies, giving rise to systemic balance-of-payments deficits and global inflation. With the century-long reign of official reserve currencies (the pound, dollar, and euro), the balance-of-payments adjustment mechanism has been consistently jammed. Thus, public finances and banking system leverage have reached astonishing crisis levels not least because balance-of-payments deficits went unsettled as reserve currency countries printed their own currencies to make payments abroad, enabling the banking system and governments to pyramid their balance sheets in a Ponzi-like scheme.

This process has led inevitably to accumulating sovereign and personal debt, accompanied by depreciating floating exchange rates, manipulated by unrestrained central bank discretion. In addition, undervalued pegged currencies, adopted by some emerging nations to subsidize exports have intensified the threat of currency wars and mercantilism.

By statutory convertibility to gold, the undisciplined, virtually unlimited discretion of the Federal Reserve Board comes to an end. The financial effect is two-fold: inflationary financing of government budget and balance-of-payments deficits is forestalled while budgetary and payments equilibria over the business cycle are reinforced.

Under this Monetary Reform Plan, sovereign governments could no longer finance ever-increasing spending and budget deficits by commandeering the issuance of cheap new credit from central or commercial banks. So long as cheap, unlimited credit is freely available to the government, budget deficits will persist and grow. (See Figure 2.) *In the United States, a federal, balanced budget amendment (or statute) is entirely consistent with this Plan.* Moreover, residual balance-of-payments deficits would be settled promptly in gold. Accumulating debt leverage, currency instability, and inflation would be diminished by prompt settlements on a day-to-day basis.

Unrestricted currency convertibility to gold, without official reserve currencies, means that incipient international balance-of-payments deficits would be quickly settled in the ordinary course of business by the reciprocal self-regulating mechanism of exports and imports of goods, services, and capital among trading nations. Remaining payment imbalances, generally modest in size, would be promptly settled exclusively by gold transfers and earmarks. Historically, under the classical gold standard, residual balance-of-payments deficits were a small fraction of the total value of international trade (Rueff 1967).

B. Termination of the World Dollar Standard

The world paper dollar standard, whereby other nations accumulate depreciating dollars as their official reserves, has enabled the United States to finance at home and abroad its ever-growing budget and balance-of-payments deficits. (See Figures 2 and 3.) But prompt settlements in gold terminate this debt-accumulating process, thereby strengthening the excessively leveraged world monetary and banking system.

Moreover, stable exchange rates mitigate the destructive effects of floating exchange rates which reduce long-term international and cross-border investment and employment opportunities in nations impacted by volatile variations in the value of national paper currencies. This is so because the disorder and volatility of floating exchange rates abruptly and arbitrarily re-price the entire national production systems of participating nations. This process renders both internal and cross-border entrepreneurial and investment activities uncertain and often unproductive, causing intermittent, widespread unemployment.

Floating currencies, rising and falling at fluctuating prices, are ruled out by mutual convertibility of major national currencies to a stipulated weight unit of gold. For each gold standard country, the future purchasing power of wages, salaries, savings, and pensions is preserved. *Security of the most vulnerable in society is assisted by maintaining the long-term stable purchasing power of the currency for those on fixed incomes.*

Multilateral convertibility of major currencies to gold establishes across cultural, insulating, suspicious foreign borders a common monetary standard necessary to create the commercial incentives and prospects for trade. It is stable exchange rates which enable the free price mechanism to allocate savings and investment efficiently in all sectors of the integrated trading system. With stable currencies persisting over the long run, dishoarding and the rise of private savings from current income make immense resources available for public and private investment in needed infrastructure.

Individual prices may and should fluctuate in the market. But with the monetary standard stabilized through statutory convertibility to gold, history shows that the general price level will vary little above and below the value at *unity* of the gold monetary standard. Under multilateral gold convertibility, the general price level is necessarily contained within the gold points of the exchange rates. Under the classical gold standard, 1879-1914, exchange rates varied no more than a small fraction of one percent above and below the gold parities of mutually convertible currencies. *Given the efficiency of contemporary communications and transportation among nations, exchange rate variations should be minuscule. But today, floating exchange rates among major nations can vary as much as twenty percent in a short period. Exorbitant commercial bank fees to supply foreign currency to consumers can range up to fifteen percent. Stable exchange rates reduce these fees to the consumer, business, and pension funds.*

In this context, "***unity***" in the previous paragraph means that the monetary standard, ***one*** *dollar, is defined as an identity with **one** precise weight unit of gold.* The general price level for nonmonetary wealth is the reciprocal of unity, namely the defined stable value of one unit of the gold monetary standard. That is to say, *the price level will be stable over the long run* so long as the stipulated gold parities of the currencies are sustained. Under the true gold standard—bound by the gold points—the general price level is subjected only to limited variations annually above and below unity. In the short run, the price level may gently fall (as it did under the classical gold standard in the late nineteenth century) or gently rise (as under the classical gold standard in the first decade of the twentieth century). But, over a generation or more, the historical evidence (e.g., 1876-1914) shows that the price level remains stable—ending at a level very near where it began (Friedman and Schwartz 1963).

Why was the price level stable under the true gold standard over the long run? Long-run stability is maintained by the empirical fact that the new supply of gold relative to above ground gold stocks tends to grow, over several decades and longer, about one-and-a-half percent (1.5%) annually on average. *The growth of the above ground gold stock is directly proportional to both population growth and average growth of Gross Domestic Product (GDP) per capita. Given the vast stocks of gold on hand, very marginal increases of one to two percent (1-2%) in the supply of gold over the long run do not materially change the value of the monetary standard. Moreover, the new supply of gold is readily absorbed at the statutory price by economic growth, by saving in the market, and by the reserves of the banking system. Marginal decreases in the supply of gold are compensated by increasing incentives to discover more gold because under convertibility the relative value (or price) of gold rises relative to the general level of prices.*

C. Stabilizing Exchange Rates; Consolidating and Refunding Official Foreign Exchange Reserves

Adoption of the simple but stable monetary mechanism and rules of the true gold standard can minimize the destabilizing effects of subsidized, undervalued exchange rates which undermine national employment. Currency convertibility to gold, at currency parities mutually agreed, would restore an efficient international adjustment mechanism so that trade and debt settlements occur promptly, mitigating leverage, encouraging balanced growth of international trade and investment. Prompt settlements limit sovereign and banking system leverage forestalling incipient insolvency.

Full resumption and settlement in gold of residual international payments deficits will require consolidation and refunding of some existing official currency reserves. *Refunding official reserve currency debt will stabilize the level of the world monetary base relative to the value of goods and services available in the market at the outset of convertibility. The aim is to maintain a reasonably stable general price level after restoration of gold convertibility and reserve currency refunding.*

D. A Common, Non-national, Global Monetary Standard

As the common, impartial, international currency, the gold monetary standard restores equity to the mechanism for integrating and maintaining stable exchange rates in the international trading system. At the same time, the common, underlying monetary standard respects sovereign currency trademarks. But the so-called world dollar standard—or the euro standard, or official reserves in dollars, yen, sterling, Swiss francs, yuan, or any other presumptive reserve currency such as the credit-based SDR—is ruled out.

In a world of inflation, paper SDRs—issued by fiat at the International Monetary Fund—amount to "irrigation during the flood." They must be ruled out. Neither a complicated basket of perishable goods, nor an unstable basket of floating currencies, but instead, the simple and objective mechanisms of the gold standard restore balance in the world monetary system.

E. Coordinating International Trade

In providing a simple, overarching rule enshrined in law, mutual convertibility of national currencies to gold coordinates free and equitable international trade among the nations, limiting mercantilism and implicit trade wars promoted by floating exchange rates and undervalued exchange rates pegged to the dollar.

All standards—such as international accounting and telecommunications standards and standards of weights and measures—are rules which create permanence and trust among public and private parties upon which contracts may be executed, thereby promoting stability and the rule of law. By example, no authority may vary the value of the defined unit of measure of the thirty-six inch (36") yardstick to twenty-nine inches (29") this year, or to thirty-nine inches (39") next year; nor may governments vary the value of a unit of weight, the pound (16 ounces), to twelve ounces this year and to twenty ounces next year. Uniform standards of weights and measures—including the monetary standard—are permanently defined to insure stability and stable expectations, enabling and underwriting honest and reliable trade at home and abroad.

Thus do Sections 8 and 10 of Article 1 of the United States Constitution (see Appendix I) provide for uniform weights and measures while prohibiting states from making anything but gold and silver coin a legal tender.

F. Legal Tender Gold Coins

Legal tender gold coins should be minted in the form of standard coin for general circulation, free of taxation at any level. Standard coin, derived from fine gold, is hardened by alloy. The coin is milled on the circumferential edge to prevent clipping. Neither gold coins nor gold bullion should be restricted in the export-import trade. Wide circulation of legal tender gold coins among participants in the market is a fundamental, democratic, regulating mechanism of the sovereign people in a stable, non-inflationary monetary system. Thus, the right to own and hold gold should not be abridged. Congress shall define the content of circulating gold coin and subsidiary coinage.

G. Banking Reform

This Monetary Reform Plan establishes a disciplined, clear, and simple framework in which central and commercial banking systems could operate effectively, ruling out subsidy or taxpayer bailout for privileged financial and private market participants. *Sending millions of small businesses and families to bankruptcy court—while bailing out both foreign governments and cartelized and subsidized banks and businesses—eviscerates free and fair markets. Such a corrupt abuse of taxpayer resources destroys the confidence, incentives, and moral dispositions of all prudent and disciplined market participants.*

Transparent and reformed institutional rules of fractional-reserve banking, subject to rigorous audit and inspection, would reinforce the institutional discipline of the true gold standard, just as convertibility restrains central bank discretion. One goal should be to reform banking laws so as to hold more accountable the directors, managers, stockholders, and principals for the solvency of the institutions they own and manage. Banks are fiduciaries, not only profit seekers. As the profits rightfully belong to the owners and managers, so should the losses. In a just system of laws and accountability, there is no room for government bailouts and subsidies to the banking system which lead directly to excessive commercial bank leverage and to egregious compensation. In the case of bank insolvency, only depositors should be held harmless by the transfer of deposits by the authorities to strong, solvent banks.

Refunding and retiring existing official foreign exchange

reserves is part of the Monetary Reform Plan, a means by which to limit and stabilize total United States government debt.

In order to insure, by market means, the true savings deposits held by commercial banks, they should be walled off in bank affiliates, protected from the leverage and greater risk to depositors inherent in fractional-reserve banking and credit-creating lending operations.

Additionally, this Plan proposes to limit manipulations of central bank credit and exchange rate policy intended to gain trading or employment advantages through currency depreciation—that is, to "beggar thy neighbor" by exporting unemployment to other countries through currency depreciation and undervaluation. In principle, mutual currency convertibility to gold—without the "exorbitant privilege" and insupportable burden of official reserve currencies—establishes a necessary, self-denying ordinance by participating nations, in the interest of the common good, in order to enhance mutual prosperity and to preserve free and fair trade among sovereign nations.

How We Get from Here to There

The Monetary Reform Plan that follows does not purport to be a legal document, only its outline. The essential elements of this Plan are summarized and simplified on pages i and ii.

I. Proposed Implementation of the Monetary Reform Plan

A. Announcement of Resumption of Convertibility

On a date certain, preferably *not more* than four years from the date of the United States' Announcement of Resumption of convertibility, the United States would establish the gold value of the dollar whereby the dollar would be defined, by statute, as a certain weight unit of gold. The likely gold weight of the dollar should be announced not more than three months in advance of a staged resumption of convertibility at the statutory value. On the date certain, the statutory gold value of the dollar will have taken effect by a lawful process determined by Congress.

After the pre-resumption market-price discovery period is complete, the gold value of the dollar should be established at a level, depending on economic circumstances, not less than the weighted average of the marginal costs of worldwide gold production, measured in dollar terms, such that the level of wages would not fall. (Econometric and business statistics for this purpose are readily available.) Such a methodology would prevent incipient deflation and unemployment subsequent to resumption of convertibility. This methodology is grounded by the fact that the value of the gold monetary standard itself—after forty years of gold price suppression and inconvertible paper currencies—should be restored to a proportional level in the hierarchy of prices and wages such that the level of nominal wages does not fall.

In conjunction with the Announcement of the Monetary Reform Plan, an International Monetary Conference should be simultaneously proposed by the United States—to convene not less than twelve months after the Announcement. The Conference location should be determined by the major participating nations.

B. Invitation to the International Monetary Conference

The essential purpose of the International Monetary Conference would be to forge a binding agreement by which to establish the basis of a stable international monetary system and stable exchange rates, grounded by major nations on unrestricted, multilateral convertibility to gold at defined parities.

Official delegations should vote. Observers from other interested countries should participate in certain discussions. Voting at the conference should be weighted to some extent by relative national output, taking into account the defense contribution of each country to the maintenance of freedom of the air and sea (the substantial cost of which is indispensable in order to maintain open and peaceful global trade). Negotiations to determine weighted voting must be anticipated.

Any nation, or any group of nations participating in the Conference, by giving notice three months after convening, might proceed alone to establish the gold standard (i.e., currency convertibility to gold at a specified parity), thereafter inviting other nations to join its new gold-based monetary system on mutually agreed terms and conditions. After the establishment

of currency convertibility to gold, such nations may take
all necessary measures to ensure equitable trading relations
with countries not yet parties to the agreed terms of the gold
standard. This provision enables progress toward convertibility
by cooperating nations if the Conference is immobilized by
disagreement.

II. Purposes of the International Monetary Conference

A. Proposed Articles of the Treaty

Articles of the Treaty would set forth the principles, rights,
and duties by which nations adhering to the new international
monetary system should operate. For example:

1. The value of the currency of each country bound to
   the agreement should be set equal to an agreed weight
   unit of gold, subsequently implemented by national
   legislation. One crucial reference point for the relative
   values of currencies of nations party to the Treaty should
   be the average dollar exchange rates in the six months

preceding the final agreement to be signed by any two or all
signatories of the monetary Treaty.

During the aforementioned six-month period, an
understanding among all parties should require that
there be no unannounced, substantial currency or foreign
exchange manipulation by monetary and fiscal authorities
of the presumed signatories. Open market operations and
currency interventions by central banks or governments
should be promptly disclosed. All sales or purchases of gold
by the authorities during this period should be immediately
disclosed.

Preceding the onset of the Conference, all participating
countries should agree to disclose, at the inception of the
Conference, all official foreign exchange holdings and
gold holdings of their national authorities—including
any official foreign exchange reserves held in the private
banking system, offshore currency markets, or elsewhere.
Independent auditors and the Minister of Finance,
Secretary of the Treasury, or equivalent should certify
these disclosures. Manifest violations should disqualify

participation in the agreement unless violations are
promptly cured.

2. In all cases, the *initial reference point* by which to negotiate
national currency exchange rates should be as stated above.
However, the gold value of each national currency may be
subject to further negotiation based upon purchasing power
parity (PPP) considerations, determined by the average
cost of production in each nation of commonly traded,
standardized, manufactured goods and services, which can
be statistically compared among the national signatories.
The convertibility price of each national currency (i.e., the
weight unit of gold by which the currency is defined by
national statute) should be agreed such that the average
level of wages in participating nations may not decline.
(Econometric analyses of comparative wage rates are
available.)

   Upon implementation of the Treaty, these tests will have
been designed to assure equitable, stable, currency exchange
rates convertible to gold.

3. *The stipulated exchange rates among the currencies for all signatories, after the effective date of the Treaty, would be explicit functions of the respective, defined gold values of their currencies. This is the necessary, enduring mark of the true gold standard and stable exchange rates—without reserve currency privileges.* Mutual convertibility of these national currencies to the common monetary standard, namely gold, should become unrestricted on a future date certain.

   In sum, *the reference points* by which to establish the gold-currency parities among the Treaty signatories should be as follows: (1) the average of the unmanipulated market exchange rates of the six months preceding the Treaty agreement; and, (2) PPP comparisons of the currencies, calculated on the basis of statistical evidence drawn from data on the average cost of commonly traded, standardized, manufactured goods and services—(net of all taxes and freight) freely available in world trade.

4. Elaborate preparations, research, and staffing having been made (during the period after the Announcement and

preceding the Conference), the conferees should produce an agreement not more than twelve months after inception. The signatories would have at least twelve additional months in which to gain approval of their legislatures and heads-of-state, but, preferably, not more than four years from the Announcement date of the Monetary Reform Plan.

If the United States were the organizer of the Conference, it may proceed independently, with notice, three months after the Announcement of the Plan, upon a finding that the Conference will not take place or will not make progress as scheduled.

5. The Treaty should take effect for each signatory, or several of them (or any one of them, alone), upon the duly approved legislation of each national government. Facts and circumstances may suggest that the conference be permitted, by mutual consent, to continue for not more than one additional year from the initial Announcement date.

All provisions of this Monetary Reform Plan to the contrary notwithstanding, no limitation—other than prudent consideration for the other conferees—is implied on the freedom of any nation to proceed alone to convertibility.

B. Proposed Collateral Agreements

The following proposals may guide unilateral convertibility rules and/or addenda to the Treaty (or treaties) in order to sustain and extend convertibility and to reinforce the liquidity of bank fiduciaries:

1. Concurrent with the effective date of the Treaty, or upon unilateral adoption of the gold standard by the United States, future *official* settlement of *residual* international payments deficits should be made only in gold. Once the United States proceeds to convertibility alone, only gold may settle residual payment imbalances of the United States with its trading partners.

2. Under the Treaty, or upon unilateral United States convertibility, official foreign exchange reserves, held in dollars, should not increase from the existing level. After a defined period, and after refunding (see pages 62-63), foreign currency reserves (or unsettled balances) should be limited to a maximum of twelve months of imports. There should be no such limitation on gold reserves. Gold should be the sole official settlement currency of residual payment imbalances after resumption of convertibility—by Treaty, or after resumption by several nations, or by the United States alone.

The true gold standard should become the cornerstone of international trade, the financial system, and the credit and banking system.

As a result of the restoration of the cornerstone in the framework of the monetary system, net new receipts of gold (or purchases) by United States monetary authorities, adding to the existing stock of gold reserves, should be accompanied by the issue of (or payment in) convertible domestic currency or bank deposits. These currency payments may not be held as official dollar reserves in foreign countries. Net outflows of official gold reserves should be associated with a reduction by like amount in the growth of United States domestic credit. Such a balancing process stabilizes the value of the currency and the general price level. (So-called sterilization procedures should be limited by Treaty and by domestic regulation.)

If several major nations proceed together to convertibility, sterilization techniques designed to forestall necessary, desirable, and balancing effects of gold transfers among nations should be prohibited. Gold transfers are the indispensable, equilibrating, balance-of-payments adjustment mechanism.

3. In the central banks of issue, or of the monetary authorities, official foreign currency reserves in excess of twelve months of import payments, after refunding, should be replaced gradually (by a date certain) either with gold or with the highest-quality, secured, short-term, private market, financial claims, denominated only in domestic currencies.

Liquidity is thereby assured.

A part of the residual official reserve claims in foreign currencies should, by conference Treaty, be refunded and amortized over time, typically a thirty-year term, at an interest rate equivalent to the loan rate of gold in the market. The consolidation of official foreign exchange reserves—to be refunded with scheduled payments—will require a sinking fund, the sums to be escrowed at the Bank for International Settlements.

4. The determination of that part of excess official foreign exchange reserves in dollars to be redeemed in gold or refunded would be at least equal to the increased value of gold holdings, at convertibility—this final sum to be determined as an amount by which the statutory currency convertibility price of gold (e.g., $3,000) exceeds the market price of gold (e.g., $2,000) on the day of the Announcement of the Monetary Reform Plan. *There should be no presumption of the convertibility price until the market discovery and clearing interval is complete (preferably less than*

four years after Announcement) and PPP considerations have been taken into account.

The aim of the verbal equation above—by which to determine the refunding schedule and termination of that excess fraction of official foreign exchange reserves by each nation—is to stabilize the total gold and foreign exchange value of the official reserves of the respective banking systems (i.e., the world monetary base)—upon the effective date of the Treaty. By this refunding technique, the goal should be to stabilize the world monetary base to assure a reasonably stable, long-term, global price level and stable exchange rates.

5. On the effective date of the Treaty, anticipating national convertibility law (after a specified adjustment period), all signatories, or the United States alone, should prohibit any further purchase by their credit-creating banking systems of any security issues of any national government, or any government affiliate, or any sub-jurisdiction thereof. This rule should apply directly to the fractional-reserve, credit-

creating segment of the banking system and to central banks. Renewed government discipline, reduced leverage, and reduced government debt with balanced budgets would be the goals.

All debt financing by government authorities should be funded outside the credit-creating banking system; that is, in the market for true domestic or international savings. Such a policy would reinforce a balanced budget statute or amendment. By means of this requirement, government-caused inflation is forestalled because governments would have no access to inflationary new issues of credit and money from the banking system.

No credit-creating central bank of signatory nations (or of that one nation proceeding to convertibility) should purchase the issues of any domestic or foreign government, or any of its sub-jurisdictions. That is, no signatory would make any further purchase, after the effective date of the Treaty (or the date of statutory convertibility) of any government securities of any country whatsoever for official reserves. The sole exception may be government tax anticipation bills, which should be certified as true taxes to be received within a twelve-month period, such government credit to be promptly repaid. Governments would have contingent access to the market for true savings.

Inasmuch as this restriction of bank-credit financing to any government jurisdiction applies strictly to the credit-creating mechanism of a leveraged, fractional-reserve banking system, the segregated true savings deposits of commercial banks should be walled off legally into an affiliate fiduciary, unencumbered by the risk of the credit-creating bank to which such restriction applies.

This restriction derives its merits from the fact that private market transactions, executed by cash or private market credit, do not produce sustained inflation. Any permanent unpaid settlement balances in the free, private market should lead by contract to liquidation or bankruptcy and, therefore, to equilibrium between the quantity of money in circulation and the desire of market participants to hold it. When there is no excess, undesired money in the market, there can be no sustained inflation.

On the other hand, new issues of credit and money, extended by the central bank or commercial banks to governments in fiscal deficit, lead to inflation since such new credit is not associated, in the same market period, with the production of new goods and services. When the government in deficit spends the newly created money on limited goods and services produced by the private market, the combined spending by government and private entities necessarily exceeds the value of those goods and services at prevailing prices. Consequently, the price level must rise as the total nominal value of spending (demand) exceeds the total value of private market production (supply). Moreover, if rising government deficits continue to be financed at home and abroad with newly created credit issued by domestic and foreign central and commercial banks, general inflation becomes systemic and sustained at fully employed resources—inducing thereby a precipitous decline of the exchange rate.

Within strict liquidity limits—set by prudence and regulation—the investment of true savings entrusted to insurance companies, money market funds, and other non-bank financial institutions may be allocated, up to a strict limit, to the highest-quality government securities of more than one-year maturity.

Defined Basel II and Basel III equity-to-asset capital ratios and defined liquidity ratios for all banks should be reinforced by national authorities at conservative levels in order to reduce the leverage and perennial abuse by bankers of the fractional-reserve banking system.

Bankers have been made unaccountable as fiduciaries by the limited liability of the corporate form. Moreover, the banking system has been subsidized by deposit insurance, cheap central bank financing, and uncompensated bailouts by American taxpayers. These subsidies have led to cartelization of the contemporary banking system, as well as irresponsible leverage and exorbitant, short-term compensation of bank executives without full accountability for the consequences of their decisions. The ever-increasing growth of mega-banks and their symbiotic mega-government patrons justifies strict regulation to enforce prudential rules.

At the minimum, a substantial portion of the short-term liabilities of the credit-creating banks should be covered by cash equivalents, or short-term, liquid, fully-secured and guaranteed commercial bills. The test of liquidity is whether such defined bank assets can be promptly sold or realized under stress—at the same value in the free market at which they were purchased. Depositors are thereby reassured. Liquidity in general and asset-equity capital ratios in particular, should take into account all fair market asset and liability values, including all derivative contracts. Banks should not rely for liquidity day-to-day on the so-called federal funds market.

The liquidity of the totality of each commercial bank portfolio would be subject to much stricter examination, the results published quarterly to show liquidation values under potential severe stress of an intensified demand for cash balances from depositors and other creditors.

III. Means of Adoption

A. Adoption by Other Nations

Without prejudice, any and all provisions of the announced Monetary Reform Plan may be carried out independently by any one or several nations. Such action by any one country should not constitute an exclusive initiative, the way remaining open for all countries to join the Monetary Reform Plan, under terms and conditions agreed by those (or the one) who have (has) implemented the Plan.

The goal is to have most members of the world community of nations join the new, stable, international monetary system on mutually agreed terms. *However, in order to make progress toward that goal, one major nation may have to lead, proceeding to complete over time the statutory and regulatory arrangements which give effect to currency convertibility to gold, including ruling out by negotiation with other nations the use of official reserve currencies in monetary and fiscal policy.*

The United States may be the one to lead by resumption of dollar convertibility to gold, holding open for an extended period access to a Treaty by other potential signatory nations.

B. The Monetary Reform Plan under American Leadership

The United States may implement the Monetary Reform Plan at its own pace, or implement a part thereof, especially if the International Monetary Conference is delayed, or if none of the major countries desires to participate immediately.

In order to implement the Plan alone, the United States should define certain terms and conditions on which, in the future, it will proceed in international trade and finance, *after* convertibility has been established. Some elements of the announced Plan may not be enacted at once. *Under these circumstances, resumption of convertibility by the United States would take place gradually during a defined and staged resumption period.*

Any foreign nation which is not a signatory to the proposed United States Monetary Reform Plan, when effective, should be subject to all sovereign United States policies needed to prevent unfair exchange rate or trade manipulations by foreign governments of the new, convertible dollar-gold parity. Manipulations deemed inequitable for the American workforce, its businesses, and government should be monitored by the authorities and regulated by countervailing United States policies.

C. Proposed Collateral Agreements

1. Upon convertibility, after an adjustment period, central
    banks should cease open market manipulations in
    currencies and domestic or international securities. *In a
    free and open market with flexible prices, the Federal Reserve
    should no longer have the authority to fix security prices at
    which to make purchases at guaranteed prices for privileged
    dealers in the bond market, or to fix the price of the so-called
    federal funds rate by which to subsidize the banks. With
    notification to Congress and the President, the Federal Reserve
    via the discount (lending) window may provide emergency
    funding to solvent banks at above-market rates, secured by
    short-duration, high-quality, liquid collateral.*

    Notification by the Federal Reserve enables appropriate
    oversight by officials directly responsible to the citizenry,
    but notice should not delay liquidity in panic periods
    which should always be fully secured by high-quality
    collateral. Emergency funding to any single institution
    should be limited by law or regulation to not more than
    six months, in aggregate, after which time the institution

will be required to issue additional equity, merge, sell, or liquidate in the event it remains unable to obtain permanent funding from private capital providers in the market.

This approach permits the central bank to provide a short-term funding facility to solvent banks during financial stress or panics. At the same time, much deeper liquidity requirements of banks should be required to reinforce stronger capital ratios and support regulations related to leverage, including all derivatives. *Such reform should create a less crisis-prone banking system, a more resilient financial system leading to more accurate market-price signals, and more moderate business cycles.*

The process whereby Congress fails to carry out much of its constitutional duty by carefully defined law allows delegated authorities, such as the Federal Reserve, too much discretion to make rules that insiders, i.e., the banks and other regulated entities, co-opt for self-serving purposes— e.g., reckless, over-leveraged, profiteering, and excessive compensation.

2. To uphold a more efficient and equitable free market financial system and the stability of exchange rates—also free from government manipulation—central banks should deploy only variations in the level of the discount rate by which to manage their portfolios during general and normal operations—discounting (or lending) freely on good collateral of non-government issues (that is, secured, liquid, financial claims of not more than one-year maturity, collateralized and co-signed by a solvent enterprise and its bank).

    Such a prudent policy insures bank liquidity and helps to forestall panic in the banking system because such liquid assets can be resold promptly in the market for the same value at which they were purchased—and thus redeemed by depositors on demand. Such bank portfolio liquidity assures the capacity to meet unanticipated demands for cash—without subsidies from the government or central bank. Thus, depositors, savers, and creditors gain confidence and trust in cash payments, in extremis, from their fiduciaries—the banks.

In a free market the true and stable goal of bank credit
policy, with or without a central bank, is not only to profit
but also to balance the supply of money in the market with
the desire of the participants to hold it so that sustained
inflation and deflation are ruled out. Sustained undesired cash
balances cause inflation. Sustained insufficient cash balances
relative to the desire to hold them leads to deflation. When
the quantity of money in circulation is equal to the desire of
market participants to hold it, the price level tends to remain
reasonably stable. This equilibrium goal is achieved if the
central bank's discount (or lending) rate is held above the
market rate, decreasing the supply of money and credit when
inflation develops. Conversely, if the discount rate is lowered
to, or below, the money market rate when the general price
level is falling, the supply of money and credit from the banks is
increased. The falling price level is thereby arrested.

Without excess money issued by the central bank to the
market, there can be no persistent rise in the price level. Nor
can there be persistent deflation when the credit policy at
the central bank aims to supply credit, on good and liquid

collateral, during disinflationary periods, at or below the money market rate.

Such a monetary policy aims at less volatility and long-run stability of exchange rates and the general price level.

The clarity and simplicity of the central bank discount rate is scaled to the modest wit of man, whereas effective open market operations require unavailable, definitive supply and demand information of the money market, as well as the impossible foresight to know the manifold arbitrage effects of central bank open market price fixing operations in the bond and currency markets.

A collateral purpose of using the discount rate (lending rate) as the primary tool of central bank credit policy is to sustain a growing, self-regulating, commercial banking system dedicated to serving consumer and business customers—grounded by the gold monetary standard and strict solvency rules—paying and receiving on demand both gold bullion and standard gold coin in exchange for convertible currency notes and dollar bank deposits. Such a commercial banking system confidently lends to a growing economy—both to qualified small and large borrowers.

Though to a great extent self-regulating, the fractional reserve banking system should always be subject to the strict rule of carefully drawn law, strict rules of audit promptly reported, and to rigorous examination by trained, independent inspectors.

3. Federal Reserve Bank assets may also contain longer-term, AAA, secured commercial issues with a maturity not greater than ten years, equal to not more than ten percent of its assets, a level consistent with the incompressible part of the circulating currency.

4. Upon the effective date of a staged resumption, by the United States alone, of dollar convertibility to gold, the Federal Reserve should test the market and purchase or sell gold to the market at an adjustable convertibility price up to a limited amount. Sales of gold ought not exceed five percent (5%) of official holdings. Unrestricted resumption of convertibility of the dollar should occur at a future date

certain. During the testing period, all purchases of gold
at the convertibility price that expand the balance sheet of
the central bank in excess of three percent (3%) per annum
should be offset by sales to the market, in like amount,
from the central bank portfolio of government securities.

Each commercial bank may purchase and sell gold for
the bank's account, so long as the purchases of gold are
offset by the sale of government securities of equal value,
permanently lowering the quantity of government securities
owned.

Over time by this process, during and after resumption,
government securities will be reduced to zero in the Federal
Reserve System and in all United States fractional-reserve,
credit-creating bank portfolios. Government securities
should be replaced in bank portfolios by short-term, liquid,
secured, commercial notes or securities of businesses in the
private market, and by gold. *This process of reducing bank
credit to the government opens up substantial commercial bank
credit to both small- and medium-sized businesses, tending to
increase employment and real wages without inflation.*

Segregated commercial bank affiliates and non-bank financial institutions, accepting true savings deposits, should retain limited discretion with respect to investing in government securities provided that their duration is proportional to their liabilities.

On the convertibility date, the United States Treasury shall exchange its gold for existing Federal Reserve gold certificates at the historic value denominated on the balance sheet of the Federal Reserve (i.e., circa $11 billion).

Thereafter, the Treasury may issue negotiable Treasury certificates fully secured and segregated for the depositor by the gold equivalent.

After an extended period of adjustment, privatization of the Federal Reserve System with no monopoly privileges may be considered.

5. The Federal Reserve and the credit-creating segment of commercial banking systems should have no more than fifteen years to eliminate all government securities from their portfolios. Not inconsistent with Basel II and Basel III

ratios, defined reserves of national credit-creating banking systems should thereafter consist entirely of gold and short-term, collateralized commercial and business securities (guaranteed by the company and its bank).

Bank reserves of monetary gold and secured, liquid financial claims, saleable on the market for the value at which they were discounted (or purchased), would become a very large fraction of bank assets. Only then can banks meet substantial unexpected demands for cash without subsidized dependence on taxpayer bailouts.

A full accounting, with footnotes detailing all assets and liabilities (and contingent liabilities to which a prudent reserve rule would apply), should be published monthly in a bank balance sheet and made available to the public and all creditors and depositors.

In the case of insolvency, liquidation or bankruptcy should result—the insured depositors alone to be held harmless.

6. A constitutionally declared state of war by Congress *may* lead to emergency economic and financial measures, to be enacted by Congress—which must terminate at war's end.

IV. Institutional Monetary Reforms

A. Supervised by Congress, and according to law, the Treasury and authorized private mints should provide for the minting of congressionally approved, standard, gold coins at the stipulated conversion rate of fine gold bullion to standard coin. Mint capital should consist in one hundred percent (100%) equity—including all congressionally authorized private and government mints.

All legal tender gold coin and gold bullion and subsidiary coinage should be exempt from any and all taxes of the United States government, the territories and jurisdictions of the United States, and of the fifty states, and of their sub-jurisdictions.

The purpose of this provision is to encourage the circulation and holding of legal tender gold coins among the people of the United States—a constitutional, democratic, regulating mechanism by which to bring to bear the necessary discipline of the sovereign people on their government, and on the credit-creating system, and on the banking system in general. To this end, the banking system should, by rule or publicized practice, hold prudential levels of gold and gold coin in order to insure convertibility of demand deposits.

In such a supple constitutional monetary system, if the Federal Reserve, the banking system, or the government, even unwittingly creates inflation by issuing undesired paper or credit dollars, the people may demand standard gold coins, or gold bullion, at the mint price—thereby inducing money and credit issuers to limit the growth of money and credit in order to limit inflation, sustain solvency, and maintain the lawful gold-dollar parity.

The subtle but irresistible mechanism of convertibility assures that as incipient inflation recedes, and the price level and the exchange rate stabilize within the gold points, gold will be re-deposited in the banks in exchange for more convenient convertible currency and bank deposits. *Gold convertibility and wide circulation of legal tender gold coins*

put the ultimate regulation of the money supply in the hands of
a free people—removing it from arbitrary government control,
central bank manipulation, and control by the banking cartel.

B. After convertibility is established, further practical currency reform will be required to mitigate the past inflationary effects on the United States economy and its monetary system. Not knowing what that future price may be, suppose the dollar convertibility price, instead of $3,000, to be $2,000 per ounce (the gold value of the dollar being the defined equivalent in grains of gold). Upon the effective date of unrestricted gold convertibility, a subsequent domestic currency exchange would be enabled by legislation at a *ten-to-one ratio*. That is, $200 in "new" convertible paper and credit currency would then be issued and exchanged with the owner of "old" paper currency. At the preference of the paper currency owner, he might demand one ounce of gold—either in standard gold coin, in convertible dollar deposit credits, or in dollar banknotes bearing the name "gold note." Gold-secured "certificates" may also be issued as segregated, custodied, warehouse receipts by gold depositories, authorized and inspected by the Treasury.

Thus, one-half of an ounce of gold would equal $100 of new notes or deposits; one-quarter ounce would equal $50. All paper denominations of new dollar currency should be exchanged for the old at the same ten-to-one ratio, with residual old currency notes to be used in the market at the new ratio until retired.

Subsidiary denominations of paper currency and coin would be provided for by Congress, making appropriate use of historic silver-, copper-, and nickel-based coin.

C. Subsequent to the staged convertibility date, standard gold coins (approximately ninety percent fine gold) in the value of $200, $100, $50, and $20, should, within a specified time period, become available at any authorized mint or at any bank. At first, there should be a short, defined notice period governing gold coin demands at the banks. The notice period should expire not later than full, effective,

unrestricted resumption of gold convertibility at the
final, stipulated gold value of the dollar, as determined by
congressional statute.

During the approximate four year (or preferably
shorter) discovery and adjustment period, but *before* full,
unrestricted resumption of convertibility is implemented
by the United States alone, the authorities should carefully
monitor the market, reporting regularly to Congress,
as the market adjusts in anticipation of the moment of
resumption.

Subsequent to the date certain of unrestricted
resumption of convertibility, redemption in gold of demand
deposits, bank notes, gold notes or Federal Reserve notes
should be required on demand. Failure to comply would
constitute default, subject to all remedies provided by law.

D. By Act of Congress, the Treasury should undertake federal
government mint preparations and authorize private mints,
according to law, to coin legal tender gold and subsidiary
currency. All mints should be inspected at prescribed

intervals with and without notice by trained and competent inspectors. (There are American statutory precedents by which to be guided.)

E. Counterfeiting, or false coin minting, should be punishable by penalties applicable to a Class B felony and by forfeiture of assets. Counterfeiting may also be punishable by a newly enacted, more severe, federal criminal statute.

F. If the United States implements domestic convertibility *alone,* resumption should be staged over not more than a four-year period from the Announcement date. During this period, Congress and the President should rigorously monitor the transition and, by law and regulation, cure any defects of the Monetary Reform Plan, so that unrestricted resumption on the date certain is efficient, seamless, and well-managed.

G. *Should the United States, alone, enact convertibility to gold,* any and every demand by foreign financial authorities to exchange dollars for gold should be subject to discretion by the appropriate American authorities. Such a managed process of limited resumption for foreigners by the United States authorities—during the period before and after unrestricted domestic resumption—depends, to some extent, on the timing and cooperation of each government of those foreign dollar holders seeking redemption both before and after they become signatories to the international agreement.

Any and every payment to non-signatories in gold—or in the case of unilateral resumption by the United States—should be contingent on presentation of banker authorized dollar balances, documented as to their source. In these cases, the Treasury alone may authorize payments in gold if the presenter acts for himself alone and is found to be in compliance with the laws of the United States, and with the United States terms and conditions of convertibility rules and statutes for non-signatories.

Lewis E. Lehrman
August 15, 2011

Conclusion

America and the world need a twenty-first century international gold standard. America should lead by unilateral resumption of the gold monetary standard. Unilateral resumption means that the United States dollar should be defined in federal statute as a certain weight unit of gold. The Treasury, the Federal Reserve System, and the banking system will be responsible for maintaining the gold value of the United States dollar.

All financial claims on banks and government agencies, chartered or supervised under federal law, that are payable in dollars shall be redeemable in gold at the statutory rate without restriction, demand deposits (e.g. checking accounts) to be redeemed upon demand but other dollar claims at maturity. Americans will be free to use gold and authorized, mint-issued gold coin as money, without restriction or the threat of taxation. The Treasury and authorized private mints will provide for the minting of legal tender gold coins, to be used as money, without restriction or taxation. The Board of Governors of the Federal

Reserve or any successor institution serving in a similar capacity, and all banks chartered or supervised by the United States government, or any one of its agencies, will be obliged by law to sustain the statutory dollar-gold parity and to redeem Federal Reserve notes and bank demand deposits for gold on demand.

To facilitate termination of the dollar-based reserve currency system American authorities will invite interested nations to a conference to establish a modernized international gold standard. By international gold standard it is meant that only gold—not dollars, nor any other national currency, nor so-called Special Drawing Rights (SDR)—would be the means by which nations settle their residual balance-of-payments deficits.

Acknowledgements

The outline of this Monetary Reform Plan was developed in the 1970s, discussed with President Reagan in 1983, and spelled out in books, essays, and op-ed pieces for several decades.

I am deeply grateful to my teammates who helped to bring this work to print. I am indebted and grateful to my excellent reviewers, and those with whom I collaborate on monetary reform, all of whom have been crucial in their shrewd criticisms, writings, and suggestions. I could write a page of tribute to each, space permitting. I mention here a few of the very helpful reviewers: Jeff Bell, Ralph Benko, Frank Cannon, Sean Fieler, Kelly Hanlon, Louise Lehrman, Peter R. Lehrman, Thomas D. Lehrman, Seth Lipsky, John Mueller, Kathleen Packard, Christopher Potter, and Frank Trotta. Others have been helpful with ideas or assistance: Andresen Blom, Rich Danker, Brian Domitrovic, Paul Fabra, Steve Forbes, Deja Hickcox, Charles Kadlec, Henri Pigeat, Passerose Rueff Pigeat, Judy Shelton, Steve Szymanski, and Susan Tang. Not all of them endorse every element of this Monetary Reform Plan. Several respected colleagues, in virtue of their modesty, make it a habit of insisting on anonymity.

It goes without saying there remain dozens of teachers and colleagues who have influenced my views over many years—and still do. I have not space to mention all, but I am no less indebted to each of them.

There is one outstanding teacher I must single out, Professor Jacques Rueff (1896-1978)—the great French central banker, prescient monetary economist of the twentieth century, author of the extraordinary French financial reforms which inaugurated in 1959 the Fifth Republic of France. He was and is, *in memoriam*, my most influential teacher and colleague.

More than fifty years ago, as an undergraduate, I was struck by the success, during a major financial crisis, of Professor Rueff's financial reform plan for France—fully embraced by General Charles DeGaulle, President of the Fifth Republic of France.

Jacques Rueff and I met later. He was a peerless economist and philosopher of the social order. For me, the personal and intellectual relationship was and is an enduring one.

There is one more essential credit—Louise, my bride of forty-five years who has inspired me in my every hope—faith, family, freedom, and fidelity to the Republic.

Lewis E. Lehrman
August 15, 2011

Appendix I: Excerpts from the United States Constitution
(See *italicized* sections)

Preamble

We the People of the United States, in Order to form a more perfect Union, establish Justice, insure domestic Tranquility, provide for the common defence, promote the general Welfare, and secure the Blessings of Liberty to ourselves and our Posterity, do ordain and establish this Constitution for the United States of America.

Article I - The Legislative Branch

Section 1 - The Legislature

All legislative Powers herein granted shall be vested in a Congress of the United States, which shall consist of a Senate and House of Representatives.

Section 2 - The House

The House of Representatives shall be composed of Members chosen every second Year by the People of the several States, and the Electors in each State shall have the Qualifications requisite for Electors of the most numerous Branch of the State Legislature.

No Person shall be a Representative who shall not have attained to the Age of twenty five Years, and been seven Years a Citizen of the United States, and who shall not, when elected, be an Inhabitant of that State in which he shall be chosen.

(Representatives and direct Taxes shall be apportioned among the several States which may be included within this Union, according to their respective Numbers, which shall be determined by adding to the whole Number of free Persons, including those bound to Service for a Term of Years, and excluding Indians not taxed, three fifths of all other Persons.) (The previous sentence in parentheses was modified by the 14th Amendment, Section 2.) The actual Enumeration shall be made within three Years after the first Meeting of the Congress of the United States, and within every subsequent Term of ten Years, in such Manner as they shall by Law direct. The Number of Representatives shall not exceed one for every thirty Thousand, but each State shall have at Least one Representative; and until such enumeration shall be made, the State of New Hampshire shall be entitled to chuse three, Massachusetts eight, Rhode-Island and Providence Plantations one, Connecticut five, New-York six, New Jersey four, Pennsylvania eight, Delaware one, Maryland six, Virginia ten, North Carolina five, South Carolina five and Georgia three.

When vacancies happen in the Representation from any State, the Executive Authority thereof shall issue Writs of Election to fill such Vacancies.

The House of Representatives shall chuse their Speaker and other Officers; and shall have the sole Power of Impeachment.

Section 3 - The Senate

The Senate of the United States shall be composed of two Senators from each State, (chosen by the Legislature thereof,) (The preceding words in parentheses superseded by 17th Amendment, Section 1.) for six Years; and each Senator shall have one Vote.

Immediately after they shall be assembled in Consequence of the first Election, they shall be divided as equally as may be into three Classes. The Seats of the Senators of the first Class shall be vacated at the Expiration of the second Year, of the second Class at the Expiration of the fourth Year, and of the third Class at the Expiration of the sixth Year, so that one third may be chosen every second Year; (and if Vacancies happen by Resignation, or otherwise, during the Recess of the Legislature of any State, the Executive thereof may make temporary Appointments until the next Meeting of the Legislature, which shall then fill such Vacancies.) (The preceding words in parentheses were superseded by the 17th Amendment, Section 2.)

No person shall be a Senator who shall not have attained to the Age of thirty Years, and been nine Years a Citizen of the United States, and who shall not, when elected, be an Inhabitant of that State for which he shall be chosen.

The Vice President of the United States shall be President of the Senate, but shall have no Vote, unless they be equally divided.

The Senate shall chuse their other Officers, and also a President pro tempore, in the Absence of the Vice President, or when he shall exercise the Office of President of the United States.

The Senate shall have the sole Power to try all Impeachments.

When sitting for that Purpose, they shall be on Oath or Affirmation. When the President of the United States is tried, the Chief Justice shall preside: And no Person shall be convicted without the Concurrence of two thirds of the Members present.

Judgment in Cases of Impeachment shall not extend further than to removal from Office, and disqualification to hold and enjoy any Office of honor, Trust or Profit under the United States: but the Party convicted shall nevertheless be liable and subject to Indictment, Trial, Judgment and Punishment, according to Law.

Section 4 - Elections, Meetings

The Times, Places and Manner of holding Elections for Senators and Representatives, shall be prescribed in each State by the Legislature thereof; but the Congress may at any time by Law make or alter such Regulations, except as to the Places of chusing Senators.

The Congress shall assemble at least once in every Year, and such Meeting shall (be on the first Monday in December,) (The preceding words in parentheses were superseded by the 20th

Amendment, Section 2.) unless they shall by Law appoint a different Day.

Section 5 - Membership, Rules, Journals, Adjournment

Each House shall be the Judge of the Elections, Returns and Qualifications of its own Members, and a Majority of each shall constitute a Quorum to do Business; but a smaller Number may adjourn from day to day, and may be authorized to compel the Attendance of absent Members, in such Manner, and under such Penalties as each House may provide.

Each House may determine the Rules of its Proceedings, punish its Members for disorderly Behaviour, and, with the Concurrence of two-thirds, expel a Member.

Each House shall keep a Journal of its Proceedings, and from time to time publish the same, excepting such Parts as may in their Judgment require Secrecy; and the Yeas and Nays of the Members of either House on any question shall, at the Desire of one fifth of those Present, be entered on the Journal.

Neither House, during the Session of Congress, shall, without the Consent of the other, adjourn for more than three days, nor to any other Place than that in which the two Houses shall be sitting.

Section 6 - Compensation

The Senators and Representatives shall receive a Compensation for their Services, to be ascertained by Law, and paid out of the Treasury of the United States. They shall in all Cases, except Treason, Felony and Breach of the Peace, be privileged from Arrest during their Attendance at the Session of their respective Houses, and in going to and returning from the same; and for any Speech or Debate in either House, they shall not be questioned in any other Place.

No Senator or Representative shall, during the Time for which he was elected, be appointed to any civil Office under the Authority of the United States, which shall have been created, or the Emoluments whereof shall have been encreased during such time; and no Person holding any Office under the United States, shall be a Member of either House during his Continuance in Office.

Section 7 - Revenue Bills, Legislative Process, Presidential Veto

All Bills for raising Revenue shall originate in the House of Representatives; but the Senate may propose or concur with Amendments as on other Bills.

Every Bill which shall have passed the House of Representatives and the Senate, shall, before it become a Law, be presented to the President of the United States; If he approve he shall sign it, but if not he shall return it, with his Objections to that House in which it shall have originated, who shall enter the Objections at large on their Journal, and proceed to reconsider it. If after such Reconsideration two thirds of that House shall agree to pass the Bill, it shall be sent, together with the Objections, to the other House, by which it shall likewise be reconsidered, and if approved by two thirds of that House, it shall become a Law. But in all such Cases the Votes of both Houses shall be determined by yeas and Nays, and the Names of the Persons voting for and against the Bill shall be entered on the Journal of each House respectively. If any Bill shall not be returned by the President within ten Days (Sundays excepted) after it shall have been presented to him, the Same shall be a Law, in like Manner as if he

had signed it, unless the Congress by their Adjournment prevent
its Return, in which Case it shall not be a Law.

Every Order, Resolution, or Vote to which the Concurrence
of the Senate and House of Representatives may be necessary
(except on a question of Adjournment) shall be presented to
the President of the United States; and before the Same shall
take Effect, shall be approved by him, or being disapproved by
him, shall be repassed by two thirds of the Senate and House
of Representatives, according to the Rules and Limitations
prescribed in the Case of a Bill.

Section 8 - Powers of Congress

The Congress shall have Power To lay and collect Taxes, Duties,
Imposts and Excises, to pay the Debts and provide for the common
Defence and general Welfare of the United States; but all Duties,
Imposts and Excises shall be uniform throughout the United States;
To borrow Money on the credit of the United States;
To regulate Commerce with foreign Nations, and among the
several States, and with the Indian Tribes;
To establish an uniform Rule of Naturalization, and uniform

Laws on the subject of Bankruptcies throughout the United States;

To coin Money, regulate the Value thereof, and of foreign Coin,
and fix the Standard of Weights and Measures;

To provide for the Punishment of counterfeiting the Securities
and current Coin of the United States;

To establish Post Offices and post Roads;

To promote the Progress of Science and useful Arts, by
securing for limited Times to Authors and Inventors the exclusive
Right to their respective Writings and Discoveries;

To constitute Tribunals inferior to the supreme Court;

To define and punish Piracies and Felonies committed on the
high Seas, and Offenses against the Law of Nations;

To declare War, grant Letters of Marque and Reprisal, and
make Rules concerning Captures on Land and Water;

To raise and support Armies, but no Appropriation of Money
to that Use shall be for a longer Term than two Years;

To provide and maintain a Navy;

To make Rules for the Government and Regulation of the
land and naval Forces;

To provide for calling forth the Militia to execute the Laws of the Union, suppress Insurrections and repel Invasions;

To provide for organizing, arming, and disciplining, the Militia, and for governing such Part of them as may be employed in the Service of the United States, reserving to the States respectively, the Appointment of the Officers, and the Authority of training the Militia according to the discipline prescribed by Congress;

To exercise exclusive Legislation in all Cases whatsoever, over such District (not exceeding ten Miles square) as may, by Cession of particular States, and the Acceptance of Congress, become the Seat of the Government of the United States, and to exercise like Authority over all Places purchased by the Consent of the Legislature of the State in which the Same shall be, for the Erection of Forts, Magazines, Arsenals, dock-Yards, and other needful Buildings;—And

To make all Laws which shall be necessary and proper for carrying into Execution the foregoing Powers, and all other Powers vested by this Constitution in the Government of the United States, or in any Department or Officer thereof.

Section 9 - Limits on Congress

The Migration or Importation of such Persons as any of the States now existing shall think proper to admit, shall not be prohibited by the Congress prior to the Year one thousand eight hundred and eight, but a Tax or duty may be imposed on such Importation, not exceeding ten **dollars*** for each Person.

The Privilege of the Writ of Habeas Corpus shall not be suspended, unless when in Cases of Rebellion or Invasion the public Safety may require it.

No Bill of Attainder or ex post facto Law shall be passed.

(No Capitation, or other direct, Tax shall be laid, unless in Proportion to the Census or Enumeration herein before directed to be taken.) (Section in parentheses clarified by the 16th Amendment.)

No Tax or Duty shall be laid on Articles exported from any State.

---

* The word "dollar" was used twice in the United States Constitution—here in Article I, Section 9, and again in Amendment 7. The term dollar as used here refers to the Spanish milled dollar which was the dominant precious metal money of the United States. At the time the United States Constitution was ratified, gold and silver money were preferred because of the terrible paper money inflation of the Revolutionary period preceding the new Constitution.

No Preference shall be given by any Regulation of Commerce or Revenue to the Ports of one State over those of another: nor shall Vessels bound to, or from, one State, be obliged to enter, clear, or pay Duties in another.

No Money shall be drawn from the Treasury, but in Consequence of Appropriations made by Law; and a regular Statement and Account of the Receipts and Expenditures of all public Money shall be published from time to time.

No Title of Nobility shall be granted by the United States: And no Person holding any Office of Profit or Trust under them, shall, without the Consent of the Congress, accept of any present, Emolument, Office, or Title, of any kind whatever, from any King, Prince or foreign State.

Section 10 - Powers Prohibited of States

No State shall *enter into any Treaty, Alliance, or Confederation; grant Letters of Marque and Reprisal; coin Money; emit Bills of Credit;* **make any Thing but gold and silver Coin a Tender in Payment of Debts;** *pass any Bill of Attainder, ex post facto Law, or Law impairing the Obligation of Contracts, or grant any Title of*

Nobility.

No State shall, without the Consent of the Congress, lay any Imposts or Duties on Imports or Exports, except what may be absolutely necessary for executing its inspection Laws: and the net Produce of all Duties and Imposts, laid by any State on Imports or Exports, shall be for the Use of the Treasury of the United States; and all such Laws shall be subject to the Revision and Controul of the Congress.

No State shall, without the Consent of Congress, lay any duty of Tonnage, keep Troops, or Ships of War in time of Peace, enter into any Agreement or Compact with another State, or with a foreign Power, or engage in War, unless actually invaded, or in such imminent Danger as will not admit of delay.

Article VII - Ratification Documents

The Ratification of the Conventions of nine States, shall be sufficient for the Establishment of this Constitution between the States so ratifying the Same.

done in Convention by the Unanimous Consent of the States present the Seventeenth Day of September in the Year of our

Lord one thousand seven hundred and Eighty seven and of the Independence of the United States of America the Twelfth. In Witness whereof We have hereunto subscribed our Names.

George Washington - President and deputy from Virginia

New Hampshire - John Langdon, Nicholas Gilman

Massachusetts - Nathaniel Gorham, Rufus King

Connecticut - William Samuel Johnson, Roger Sherman

New York - Alexander Hamilton

New Jersey - William Livingston, David Brearley, William Paterson, Jonathan Dayton

Pennsylvania - Benjamin Franklin, Thomas Mifflin, Robert Morris, George Clymer, Thomas FitzSimons, Jared Ingersoll, James Wilson, Gouverneur Morris

Delaware - George Read, Gunning Bedford Jr., John Dickinson, Richard Bassett, Jacob Broom

Maryland - James McHenry, Daniel of St. Thomas Jenifer, Daniel Carroll

Virginia - John Blair, James Madison Jr.

North Carolina - William Blount, Richard Dobbs Spaight, Hugh Williamson

South Carolina - John Rutledge, Charles Cotesworth Pinckney, Charles Pinckney, Pierce Butler

Georgia - William Few, Abraham Baldwin

Attest: William Jackson, Secretary

Appendix II: The Coinage Act of 1792

Chapter XVI - An Act establishing a Mint, and regulating the coins of the United States.

Section I - Mint Established at the seat of government

Be it enacted by the Senate and House of Representatives of the United States of American in Congress assembled, and it is hereby enacted and declared, That a mint for the purpose of a national coinage be, and the same is established; to be situated and carried on at the seat of the government of the United States, for the time being: And that for the well conducting of the business of the said mint, there shall be the following officers and persons, namely, —a Director, an Assayer, a Chief Coiner, an Engarver, a Treasurer.   ...

Section 9 - Species of the Coins to be Struck

And be it further enacted, That there shall be from time to time struck and coined at the said mint, coins of gold, silver, and copper, of the following denominations, values and descriptions, viz.

EAGLES—each to be of the value of ten dollars or units, and to contain two hundred and forty-seven grains and four eighths of a grain of pure, or two hundred and seventy grains of standard gold.

HALF EAGLES—each to be of the value of five dollars, and to contain one hundred and twenty-three grains and six eighths of a grain of pure, or one hundred and thirty-five grains of standard gold.

QUARTER EAGLES—each to be of the value of two dollars and a half dollar, and to contain sixty-one grains and seven eighths of a grain of pure, or sixty-seven grains and four eighths of a grain of standard gold.

DOLLARS OR UNITS—each to be of the value of a Spanish milled dollar as the same is now current, and to contain three hundred and seventy-one grains and four sixteenth parts of a grain of pure, or four hundred and sixteen grains of standard silver.

HALF DOLLARS—each to be of half the value of the dollar or unit, and to contain one hundred and eighty-five grains and ten sixteenth parts of a grain of pure, or two hundred and eight grains of standard silver.

QUARTER DOLLARS—each to be of one fourth the value of the dollar or unit, and to contain ninety-two grains and thirteen sixteenth parts of a grain of pure, or one hundred and four grains of standard silver.

DISMES—each to be of the value of one tenth of a dollar or unit, and to contain thirty-seven grains and two sixteenth parts of a grain of pure, or forty-one grains and three fifth parts of a grain of standard silver.

HALF DISMES—each to be of the value of one twentieth of a dollar, and to contain eighteen grains and nine sixteenth parts of a grain of pure, or twenty grains and four fifth parts of a grain of standard silver.

CENTS—each to be of the value of the one hundredth part of a dollar, and to contain eleven penny-weights of copper.

HALF CENTS—each to be of the value of half a cent, and to contain five penny-weights and half a penny-weight of copper.

Section 10 - Of What Devices

And be it further enacted, That, upon the said coins

respectively, there shall be the following devices and legends, namely: Upon one side of each of the said coins there shall be an impression emblematic of liberty, with an inscription of the word Liberty, and the year of the coinage; and upon the reverse of each of the gold and silver coins there shall be the figure or representation of an eagle, with this inscription, "UNITED STATES OF AMERICA" and upon the reverse of each of the copper coins, there shall be an inscription which shall express the denomination of the piece, namely, cent or half cent, as the case may require.

Section 11 - Proportional Value of Gold and Silver

And be it further enacted, That the proportional value of gold to silver in all coins which shall by law be current as money within the United States, shall be fifteen to one, according to quantity in weight, of pure gold or pure silver; that is to say, every fifteen pounds weight of pure silver shall be of equal value in all payments, with one pound weight of pure gold, and so in proportion as to any greater or less quantities of the respective metals.

Section 12 - Standard for Gold Coins, and Alloy How to be Regulated

And be it further enacted, That the standard for all gold coins of the United States shall be eleven parts fine to one part alloy; and accordingly that eleven parts in twelve of the entire weight of each of the said coins shall consist of pure gold, and the remaining one twelfth part of alloy; and the said alloy shall be composed of silver and copper, in such proportions not exceeding one half silver as shall be found convenient; to be regulated by the director of the mint, for the time being, with the approbation of the President of the United States, until further provision shall be made by law. And to the end that the necessary information may be had in order to the making of such further provision, it shall be the duty of the director of the mint, at the expiration of a year after commencing the operations of the said mint, to report to Congress the practice thereof during the said year, touching the composition of the alloy of the said gold coins, the reasons for such practice, and the experiments and observations which shall have been made concerning the effects of different proportions of silver and copper in the said alloy.

Section 13 - Standard for Silver Coins, and Alloy How to be Regulated

And be it further enacted, That the standard for all silver coins of the United States, shall be one thousand four hundred and eighty-five parts fine to one hundred and seventy-nine parts alloy; and accordingly that one thousand four hundred and eighty-five parts in one thousand six hundred and sixty-four parts of the entire weight of each of the said coins shall consist of pure silver, and the remaining one hundred and seventy-nine parts of alloy; which alloy shall be wholly of copper.

Section 19 - Penalty on Debasing the Coins

And be it further enacted, That if any of the gold or silver coins which shall be struck or coined at the said mint shall be debased or made worse as to the proportion of the fine gold or fine silver therein contained, or shall be of less weight or value than the same ought to be pursuant to the directions of this act, through the default or with the connivance of any of the officers or persons who shall be employed at the said mint, for the purpose of profit or gain, or otherwise with a fraudulent intent, and if any of the said officers or persons shall embezzle any of the metals which shall at any time be committed to their charge for the purpose of being coined, or any of the coins which shall be struck or coined at the said mint, every such officer or person who shall commit any or either of the said offences, shall be deemed guilty of felony, and shall suffer death.

Section 20 - Money of Account to be Expressed in Dollars

And be if further enacted, That the money of account of the United States shall be expressed in dollars, or units, dismes or tenths, cents or hundredths, and the milles or thousandths, a disme being the tenth part of a dollar, a cent the hundredth part of a dollar, a mille the thousandth part of a dollar, and that all accounts in the public offices and all proceedings in the courts of the United States shall be kept and had in conformity to this regulation.

Appendix III: American Monetary History in Brief—Price Stability

Monetary history suggests that a constitutional monetary reform—specifically, restoring the true gold standard without official reserve currencies will end chronic episodes of inflation (or deflation), rebalance United States international payments deficits, and limit endless Federal deficit spending.

A very brief monetary history of the United States. The stability of the United States dollar has varied widely in its history. This variation is explained by two factors: (1) the monetary standard chosen for the dollar; and, (2) whether other countries have simultaneously used cash and securities payable in dollars as their own official reserves, or as their monetary standard itself (i.e., official reserve currencies in place of domestic money).

The United States has alternated between two kinds of standard money: inconvertible paper money and some precious metal (first silver, then gold). The dollar was an inconvertible paper money during and after the Revolutionary

War (1776–92), the War of 1812 (1812–17), the Civil War and Reconstruction (1862–79), and again from 1971 to the present. The dollar was effectively defined as a weight of silver (and gold) in 1792–1812 and 1817–34 and effectively as a weight of gold in 1834–61 and 1879–1971. (The minted gold eagle, defined as ten dollars, was provided for in the Coinage Act of 1792.) The dollar was not used by foreign monetary authorities as an official monetary reserve asset before 1914, but the dollar has been an official "reserve currency" for many countries since 1914 (at first along with the British pound). The dollar has been the primary official reserve currency for most countries since 1944. Ours is the era of the world dollar standard.

Applying two criteria divides the monetary history of the United States into distinct phases. We can compare the stability of these monetary regimes by examining the variation in the Consumer Price Index (as reconstructed back to 1800) by two simple measures: long-term CPI stability (measured by the annual average change from beginning to end of the period of each monetary standard) and short-term CPI volatility (measured by the standard deviation of annual CPI changes during the period).

Weighting these criteria equally, the classical gold standard from 1879-1914 was the most stable of all United States monetary regimes (as the table below shows).

The true gold standard of this Monetary Reform Plan, fully integrated as it is with the modern credit superstructure, suggests similarities to the classical gold standard.

United States Consumer Price Index

(Long-term stability and short-term volatility, by period and monetary system: 1800-2009)

	Long-Run Stability *(Average Annual Change)*	Short-Run Volatility *(Std. Deviation Annual Change)*	Maximum Price Change *(High vs. Low)*	Stability Rank *(Weighing Both Criteria Equally)*
1800-1834 Domestic Silver Standard *(Interrupted 1812-17 by domestic paper standard)*	-1.5%	5.2%	76%	4
1834-1861 Domestic Gold Standard	-0.4%	3.5%	36%	2
1862-1879 Domestic Paper Standard	+0.1%	8.8%	74%	3
1879-1914 International Gold Standard	+0.2%	2.2%	20%	1
1914-1944 Interwar International Gold-Dollar-Sterling Standard	+1.9%	7.2%	99%	5
1944-1971 Bretton Woods International Gold-Dollar Standard	+3.1%	3.1%	130%	4
1971-2009 International Paper Dollar Standard *(1971-1981)* *(1981-2009)*	+4.5% *(+8.5%)* *(+3.1%)*	2.8% *(+2.7%)* *(+1.2%)*	432% *(125%)* *(137%)*	4

Sources and Notes: Edited and shortened by Lewis E. Lehrman from the original by John D. Mueller in *Redeeming Economics* (ISI Books, 2010).

Selected Bibliography

For the general reader, I include this modest and diverse selection of books and articles on the gold standard and monetary economics. Many longer bibliographies exist. I am indebted to many scholars, economists, and historians not included in this brief selection.

Bagehot, Walter. *Lombard Street: A Description of the Money Market.* New York, NY: E.P. Dutton, 1921.

Barro, Robert J. "Money and the Price Level under the Classical Gold Standard." *Economic Journal* 89 (1979): 13-33.

Bernanke, Ben. *Essays on the Great Depression.* Princeton, NJ: Princeton University Press, 2004.

Barnett, Correlli. *The Collapse of British Power.* Amherst, NY: Prometheus Books, 1986.

---. "Nonmonetary Effects of the Financial Crisis in the Propagation of the Great Depression." *American Economic Review* 73, no. 3 (1983): 257-276.

Bordo, Michael. *The Gold Standard and Related Monetary Regimes: Collected Essays.* Cambridge: Cambridge University Press, 1999.

Bordo, Michael, and Anna Schwartz. *A Retrospective on the Classical Gold Standard, 1821-1931.* Chicago, IL: University of Chicago Press, 1984.

Calleo, David, Charles Kindleberger, and Lewis Lehrman. *Money and the Coming World Order.* New York, NY: New York University Press, 1976. (N.B.: A project of the Lehrman Institute.)

Chappel, David, and Kevin Dowd. "A Simple Model of the Gold Standard." *Journal of Money, Credit and Banking* 29, no. 1 (1997): 94-105.

Chivvis, Christopher. *The Monetary Conservative: Jacques Rueff and Twentieth-century Free Market Thought.* DeKalb, IL: Northern Illinois University Press, 2010.

Clark, Gregory. *A Farewell to Alms: A Brief Economic History of the World.* Princeton, NJ: Princeton University Press, 2008.

Claasen, Emil-Marie and Georges Lane, eds. *Oeuvres Complètes de Jacques Rueff.* 4 vols. Paris: Plon, 1977-1981. (N.B.: A project of the Lehrman Institute.)

Cooper, Richard N., Rudiger Dornbusch, and Robert E. Hall. "The Gold Standard: Historical Facts and Future Prospects." *Brookings Papers on Economic Activity* 1982, no. 1 (1982): 1-56.

Dam, Kenneth W. "From the Gold Clause Cases to the Gold Commission: A Half Century of American Monetary Law." *University of Chicago Law Review* 50, no. 2 (1983): 504-532.

Domitrovic, Brian. *Econoclasts: The Rebels Who Sparked the Supply-Side Revolution and Restored American Prosperity.* Wilmington, DE: ISI Books, 2009.

Dubey, Pradeep, John Geanakoplos, and Martin Shubik. "Is Gold an Efficient Store of Value?" *Economic Theory* 21, no. 4 (2003): 767-782.

Eichengreen, Barry. *Golden Fetters: The Gold Standard and the Great Depression, 1919-1939.* New York, NY: Oxford University Press, 1995.

Fellner, William, Fritz Machlup, and Robert Triffin. *Maintaining and Restoring Balance in International Payments.* Princeton, NJ: Princeton University Press, 1966.

Ferguson, Niall. *The Ascent of Money: A Financial History of the World.* New York, NY: Penguin Press, 2008.

Friedman, Milton, and Anna Schwartz. *A Monetary History of the United States, 1867-1960.* Princeton, NJ: Princeton University Press, 1963.

Hayek, Friedrich. *The Road to Serfdom.* London: Routledge, 1944.

Gallarotti, Giulio. "Hegemons of a Lesser God: The Bank of France and Monetary Leadership under the Classical Gold Standard." *Review of International Political Economy* 12, no. 4 (2005): 624-646.

---. *The Anatomy of an International Monetary Regime: The Classical Gold Standard, 1880-1914.* New York, NY: Oxford University Press, 1995.

Grant, James D. *Mr. Market Miscalculates: The Bubble Years and Beyond.* Edinburg, VA: Axios Press, 2008.

---. *The Trouble with Prosperity.* New York, NY: Crown Business, 1998.

James, Harold. *International Monetary Cooperation since Bretton Woods.* New York, NY: Oxford University Press, 1996.

Jastram, Roy. *The Golden Constant: The English and American Experience, 1500-1976.* Hoboken, NJ: John Wiley and Sons, 1977.

Kenen, Peter. *British Monetary Policy and the Balance of Payments, 1951-1957.* Cambridge, MA: Harvard University Press, 1960.

Kenen, Peter and Alexander Swodoba, eds. *Reforming the International Monetary and Financial System.* Washington, D.C.: International Monetary Fund, 2000.

Keynes, John Maynard. *The General Theory of Employment, Interest, and Money.* New York, NY: Harcourt Brace and Company, 1964.

Kindleberger, Charles P. *Manias, Panics, and Crashes: A History of Financial Crises.* New York, NY: Basic Books, 1978.

---. *The World in Depression, 1929-1939.* Berkeley, CA: University of California Press: 1986.

Knafo, Samuel. "The Gold Standard and the Origins of the Modern International Monetary System." *Review of International Political Economy* 13, no. 1 (2006): 78-102.

Lehrman, Lewis. "China: American Financial Colony or Mercantilist Predator." *The American Spectator* (September 2011): 28-32.

---. "The Dollar Problem and Its Solution." *The Intercollegiate Review* (Fall 2011): 3-10.

---. *Gold in a Global Multi-Asset Portfolio.* New York, NY: Morgan Stanley and Company, 1988.

---. *Lincoln at Peoria: The Turning Point.* Mechanicsburg, PA: Stackpole Books, 2008.

---. *Monetary Policy, the Federal Reserve, and Gold.* New York, NY: Morgan Stanley and Company, 1980.

---. *Protectionism, Inflation, or Monetary Reform: The Case for Fixed Exchange Rates and a Modernized Gold Standard.* New York, NY: Morgan Stanley and Company, 1985.

---. "To Move Forward, Go Back to Gold." *New York Times,* February 9, 1986, national edition, sec. "Week in Review." (N.B.: This article was an early precursor to this Monetary Reform Plan.)

---. *Whither Gold?* New York, NY: Morgan Stanley and Company, 1989.

Mises, Ludwig von. *The Anti-capitalistic Mentality.* Indianapolis, IN: Liberty Fund, 2006.

---. *Human Action: A Treatise on Economics.* New Haven, CT: Yale University Press, 1949.

Mueller, John D. *Redeeming Economics, Rediscovering the Missing Element.* Wilmington, DE: ISI Books, 2010.

Mundell, Robert A. *Man and Economics.* Columbus, OH: McGraw-Hill, 1968.

---. *Monetary Theory: Inflation, Interest and Growth in the World Economy.* Pacific Palisades, CA: Goodyear Publishing Company, 1971.

Paul, Ron, and Lewis Lehrman. *The Case for Gold*. Washington, D.C.: Cato Institute, 1982.

Pietrusza, David. *It Shines for All: The Gold Standard Editorials of the New York Sun*. New York, NY: New York Sun Books, 2011.

Reinhart, Carmen M. and Kenneth S. Rogoff. *This Time Is Different: Eight Centuries of Financial Folly*. Princeton, NJ: Princeton University Press, 2009.

Röpke, Wilhelm. *A Humane Economy: The Social Framework of the Free Market*. Wilmington, DE: ISI Books, 1999 (3rd edition).

Romer, Christina. "The Nation in Depression." *Journal of Economic Perspectives* 7, no. 2 (1993): 19-39.

Rothbard, Murray. *A History of Money and Banking in the United States: The Colonial Era to World War II*. Auburn, AL: Ludwig von Mises Institute, 2002.

Rowland, Benjamin, ed. *Balance of Power or Hegemony: The Interwar Monetary System*. New York, NY: New York University Press, 1976. (N.B.: A project of the Lehrman Institute.)

Rueff, Jacques. *The Age of Inflation*. Washington, DC: Henry Regnery and Company, 1964.

---. *The Balance-of-payments: Proposals for Resolving the Critical World Economic Problem of our Time*. New York, NY: Macmillan, 1967.

---. *From the Physical to the Social Sciences: An Introduction to the Study of Economic and Ethical Theory*. Washington, D.C.: The Johns Hopkins University Press, 1929.

---. *The Gods and the Kings: A Glance at Creative Power.* New York, NY: Macmillan, 1973.

---. *The Monetary Sin of the West.* New York, NY: Macmillan, 1979.

Rueff, Jacques, and Fred Hirsch. *The Role and The Rule of Gold: An Argument.* Princeton, NJ: Princeton University Press, 1965.

Schwartz, Anna. "Reflections on the Gold Commission Report." *Journal of Money, Credit, and Banking* 14, no. 4, part 1 (1982): 538-551.

Shlaes, Amity. *The Forgotten Man: A New History of the Great Depression.* New York, NY: Harper Collins, 2007.

Skidelsky, Robert. *John Maynard Keynes.* 3 vols. New York, NY: Basic Books, 1983, 1995, 2002.

Smith, Adam. *An Inquiry into the Nature and Causes of the Wealth of Nations.* Edited by R.H. Campbell and A.S. Skinner. Indianapolis, IN: Liberty Fund, 1982.

Tasca, Diane. *U.S.-Japanese Economic Relations: Co-Operation, Competition, and Confrontation.* Elmsford, New York: Pergamon Press, 1980. (N.B.: A project of the Lehrman Institute.)

Temin, Peter. *Did Monetary Forces Cause the Great Depression?* New York, NY: W.W. Norton and Company, 1975.

Triffin, Robert. *Europe and the Money Muddle: From Bilateralism to Near-Convertibility, 1947-1956.* Westport, CT: Greenwood Press, 1957.

---. *The Evolution of the International Monetary System: Historical Reappraisal and Future Perspectives.* Princeton, NJ: Princeton Studies in International Finance, 1964.

---. *Gold and the Dollar Crisis: The Future of Convertibility.* New Haven, CT: Yale University Press, 1966.

---. *Our International Monetary System: Yesterday, Today, Tomorrow.* New York, NY: Random House, 1968.

---. *The World Money Maze: National Currencies in International Payments.* New Haven, CT: Yale University Press, 1966.

Tucker, Robert. *The Atlantic Alliance and Its Critics.* Westport, CT: Praeger Publishers, 1983. (N.B.: A project of the Lehrman Institute.)

---. *The Purposes of American Power: An Essay on National Security.* Westport, CT: Praeger Publishers, 1981. (N.B.: A project of the Lehrman Institute.)

United States Congress. House Committee on Financial Services. *The Relationship of Monetary Policy and Rising Prices.* 112th Cong., 1st sess., March 17, 2011. Testimony by Lewis E. Lehrman.

Index